The Roman Empire

A Beginner's Guide

ONEWORLD BEGINNER'S GUIDES combine an original, inventive, and engaging approach with expert analysis on subjects ranging from art and history to religion and politics, and everything in-between. Innovative and affordable, books in the series are perfect for anyone curious about the way the world works and the big ideas of our time.

The Roman Empire
A Beginner's Guide

Philip Matyszak

ONEWORLD

A Oneworld Paperback Original

Published in North America, Great Britain and Australia by
Oneworld Publications 2014

ISBN 978-1-78074-424-7
eISBN 978-1-78074-425-4

Typeset by Siliconchips Services Ltd, UK
Printed and bound by
Nørhaven, Denmark

Oneworld Publications
10 Bloomsbury Street
London WC1B 3SR
England

Contents

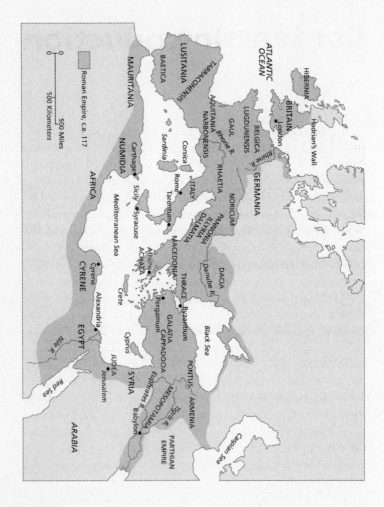

ATLANTIC OCEAN

HIBERNIA

BRITAIN
• London

Hadrian's Wall

LUSITANIA
BAETICA
TARRACONENSIS
MAURITANIA

AQUITANIA
NARBONENSIS
GAUL
LUGDUNENSIS
BELGICA
GERMANIA
Rhine R.
Rhône R.
RHAETIA
NORICUM

NUMIDIA
Carthage
Sardinia
Corsica
Rome
ITALY
Tarentum
Sicily
Syracuse

AFRICA

Mediterranean Sea

PANNONIA
DALMATIA
ILLYRIA
MACEDONIA
ACHAEA
Athens
Crete
Pergamum
THRACE
Byzantium
DACIA
Danube R.
Black Sea

CYRENE
Cyrene
Alexandria
EGYPT
Nile R.
Red Sea

GALATIA
CAPPADOCIA
Cyprus
JUDEA
Jerusalem
SYRIA
PONTUS
ARMENIA
MESOPOTAMIA
Euphrates R.
Tigris R.
Babylon
PARTHIAN EMPIRE
Caspian Sea

ARABIA

Roman Empire, c.a. 117

500 Miles
0
500 Kilometers
0

Introduction

In 612 BCE, a great empire came to an end. At its height the Assyrian Empire had dominated Asia Minor, ruled Egypt and established provinces deep in what is today Iran. Yet its end was dramatic and bloody. A confederation of subject peoples, led by the city-state of Babylon, fell upon Nineveh, Assyria's capital city. When Nineveh fell, the empire's vengeful former vassals took the city apart brick by brick and massacred the inhabitants. Assyria's empire was snuffed out and Nineveh lay abandoned and desolate for centuries.

The Assyrians, as had all conquerors before them, had made a clear distinction between conquerors and conquered: the conquered served the conquerors and existed on their sufferance. At the time no one paid much attention to an almost unprecedented development far away on the barbaric western fringe of the known world. The small city-state of Rome, founded some 150 years before Nineveh's fall, chose a radical new approach. Rome had a desperate shortage of manpower and an abundance of enemies, so the little state (only about forty kilometres across at the time) either had to attempt innovative measures or be overwhelmed by the more numerous, and highly predatory, cities and tribes of central Italy.

Rome's response was typically pragmatic: if Rome lacked resources, the solution was to have more Rome. The city became aggressively expansionist. While Assyria was being demolished by subjects who were not Assyrian and had never felt Assyrian, Roman tradition tells us that King Tarquin the Elder was conquering the people of Apiolae. (Conquest of the cities of Camerina,

Corniculum and Nomentum soon followed.) However, Tarquin made the conquered people not Roman *subjects* but Roman *citizens*. Rome had made a conceptual breakthrough: the citizens of a city need not live in that city. They could live hundreds of kilometres away, be active in the affairs of a city that they and their families regarded as home, yet still be Roman citizens. In time, these new Roman citizens became the equals of their conqueror; not merely loyal subjects but as Roman in thought and deed as anyone born on Rome's seven hills.

As Rome expanded to become an Italian and then a Mediterranean power, the innate conservatism of later Romans meant that they were slow to abandon the policies of their ancestors. More and more conquered peoples were absorbed into the Roman state as Romans. The city of Arpinum, in Latium, was captured by Rome in 305 BCE and its inhabitants immediately made citizens, although not given the vote. (Full suffrage was granted in 188 BCE.) Caius Marius, a native of Arpinum, became consul of Rome several times over and led Roman armies to victory in Africa and Gaul. In 63 BCE, another Arpinate, Marcus Tullius Cicero, became consul of Rome, never thinking of himself as anything but a fully Roman citizen.

By the time of the first Roman emperors, conquest by absorption had become an explicit doctrine. The historian Tacitus (in *Annals* 11.24) records this speech made by the emperor Claudius in 48 CE:

> What ruined Sparta and Athens, but this? They were mighty in war, but they rejected as aliens those whom they had conquered. Totally different was our father Romulus, who in his wisdom fought [the people of] several nations as enemies and then greeted them as fellow-citizens, all on the same day. We have been ruled by foreigners. The sons of freed slaves have been trusted with public office. And do not think this is something new in our time – it was common practice of old ... Now they are united with

us in culture, education and intermarriage, let them bring us their gold and their wealth rather than enjoying it by themselves.

The Mediterranean world became a vast social experiment. From the Thames to the Tigris, peoples, who a few generations before had been only vaguely aware of each other's existence, were now united as members of a single empire. Over the next five hundred years these peoples came together in religion, language and culture to form a society that largely still exists today. Westerners find Rome in their vocabulary (such as in the word 'romance'), in the architecture of their civic buildings and in the political and legal structures that govern their daily lives.

The contrast with Assyria could not be more dramatic. When the Roman Empire in the west collapsed in the fifth century CE, the peoples of the Greek east did not join in the assault on Rome, nor did they wish to eradicate the empire. They had no interest in throwing off the shackles of Roman oppression, because they had become Romans. The emperor in the Greek east still consulted his senate, chariots continued to race in the circus and the laws of Rome remained the law of the land. For another thousand years, Rome's empire lived on among the peoples the city had conquered.

How this came to be is the story told in this book. The story of how one kind of Roman empire, an empire ruled by Romans, became a completely different kind of Roman empire: an empire *of* Romans. This story focuses not on the city of Rome, not on the antics of the imperial court, nor even on the many wars which Rome fought with neighbouring states. Instead, its emphasis lies on the provinces which made up the empire. There, a slow sea-change took sullen, conquered peoples and made them contributors to and partners in a civilisation so dynamic and vibrant that it survived the collapse of Roman military and civic power to become the foundation of the Europe we know today.

1

Rome in the Republic: an empire without an emperor

Rome conquered most of the lands that made up its empire while the state was still a republic. Almost from the time it was founded, the Roman state began absorbing neighbouring peoples and cities. As Rome grew stronger, more resources became available for military operations and the pace of conquest accelerated. During the later years of the Republic it was not unusual for several kingdoms to fall under Román control in a single year. Though there were substantial additions in the imperial period, it is fair to say that by the time Augustus became Rome's first emperor, much of Rome's empire was largely in place. Under Augustus, the limits of Roman power lay at the waters of the Euphrates River in the east and at the beaches of Gaul in the west.

Between these two points, four thousand kilometres apart, was an empire of millions of people, living in hundreds of cities, in environments that ranged from desert sands and mountains to pine forests and bogs. All that the subjects of Rome's growing empire had in common was that they had submitted to the power of the Roman legions. In religion, architecture, art, language, society and culture, the peoples of Rome's new empire were considerably more different from each other than they were from their neighbours just beyond the frontier.

When Augustus became Rome's first emperor in 31 BCE, few of the natives of the provinces he ruled thought of themselves as

Romans. With the passing of the centuries, much would change. A time would come when the city of Rome was not the centre of imperial government; and eventually the empire would be divided. The peoples of the east would continue to call themselves 'Roman' long after Rome had fallen to the barbarians. Between the reigns of Rome's first and last emperors a slow fusion of Latin, Greek and Gallic cultures took place. The physical conquest of the Mediterranean world was only the first stage in the creation of a truly Roman empire; an empire which would, largely, remain even when the bonds of political and military control had fallen away. This chapter examines how Rome came to master the Mediterranean world and how the government coped with the challenge of ruling what was originally a hugely diverse mass of peoples. Understanding the empire of the Caesars requires us to understand the Republican empire from which it evolved and an understanding of the institutions of the Republic that the Caesars usurped.

Acquiring an empire

> Who among men is so ignorant or lazy that he does not want to know how and by what sort of government almost everything in the world was conquered and fell under the sole rule of the Romans?
>
> Introductory remarks by Polybius, *History* 1.1.5

The origins of the city of Rome are shrouded in the mists of legend. Whatever details of this legend may be disputed, no one denies that, once the city had been founded some time in the eighth century BCE, the Romans had to fight for their existence. It is significant that in the foundation legend Romulus' first act was to build a defensive wall. The Romans expected to be attacked and they were. The new city arose at the lowest bridgeable (or fordable) point of the Tiber, sitting squarely across an already ancient trade route. This was the *via Salaria*, which, as its name suggests, was the route by which salt was carried from the salt flats of the coast to the Italian interior.

Romulus and Remus

The legend of Rome's most famous twins tells us much of how the Romans saw themselves and their origins. The mother of the twins was Rhea Silva, a member of the royal family of the city of Alba Longa, who was made a Vestal Virgin by a usurping relative. This move was meant to prevent Rhea from having children, so when she became pregnant this meant her execution. Some forms of the legend claim that the king deliberately raped Rhea, wearing a helmet to avoid being recognised.

If so, the plan backfired, because Rhea deftly claimed that the father of the twins was the war god, Mars himself. This idea gained enough popular support to save Rhea's life but the king ordered the newborn children to be thrown into the swollen river Tiber. A kindly servant put the twins into a basket. When this floated ashore, the pair were found and suckled by a she-wolf who had lost her cubs. Adopted later by a shepherd, the pair grew up unaware of their origins. When they did discover their royal birth, they marched on Alba Longa and overthrew the usurper king. However, the twins decided to found a city of their own.

The site was the subject of debate. Eventually, Romulus had his way and began building walls on the Palatine hill. When Remus mocked his efforts by vaulting the earthworks, he was slain by a furious Romulus. Once his city was established, Romulus ruled as king. At the end of his rule, he mysteriously vanished – either taken up to the heavens as a god, or killed by senators, who smuggled away his body parts under their togas.

This story shows the Romans having their cake and eating it. Their origins are noble – a princess and a god – but simultaneously humble; shepherd boys possibly raised by a prostitute (*lupa* means either she-wolf or prostitute). The birth of Rome is both divinely ordained and founded on blood and murder. Finally, Romulus either became a god (worshipped as Quirinus) or was justly assassinated for his increasingly despotic ways. So the Romans could claim both to have started from nothing, and also with divine and noble origins.

Furthermore, Rome was founded on the border between Latium and Etruria and relations between the Latins and Etruscans were generally fraught and often violent. Add marauding hill tribes and the fact that Rome had annexed the Capitoline Hill (which was already a site of considerable religious significance) and it becomes clear that the Romans could expect to do even more fighting than the considerable amount customary for contemporary Italian city-states.

Rome developed a warrior culture 'strong and disciplined by the lessons of war' as Livy puts it (1.21.5). Legend records wars with the neighbouring Sabine and Latin peoples and also conflicts with the nearby cities of Fidenae and Veii. Archaeology and legend alike strongly suggest a period of Etruscan dominance, though it should be remembered that like the Greeks, the Etruscans lived in city-states that fought each other as much as their external enemies. Even Etruscan-dominated Rome probably allocated part of the campaigning season to fighting Etruscans.

The militaristic culture of Rome developed alongside Rome itself. This warlike ethos was to remain dominant well after the end of the Republic. A linked trend – and another key factor in the development of Rome – was that from the very beginning Rome was relentlessly expansionist. Legend tells us that Rome accepted refugees, men fleeing justice and escaped slaves in equal measure, kidnapping wives for them from the neighbouring Sabine tribe. The historical record concurs; by the time fact becomes distinct from legend, the coastal city of Ostia was already Roman, the Sabine people had been assimilated and a number of adjoining cities, possibly including Alba Longa, Rome's mother-city, had been conquered. Often, the populations of these conquered cities were forcibly translocated to Rome.

When Tarquin the Proud, Rome's last king, was expelled in 508 BCE, Rome was a tidy but relatively small city state at most fifty kilometres in breadth. It was possible for a man fighting

The seven kings of Rome

Romulus	763–716 BCE
Numa Pompilius	716–674 BCE
Tullus Hostilius	674–642 BCE
Ancus Martius	641–617 BCE
Tarquin the elder	617–579 BCE
Servius Tullius	579–535 BCE
Tarquin the Proud	535–508 BCE

The number seven was highly symbolic in the classical world: there were seven wonders, seven sages and of course seven hills of Rome (which could easily have been any number from five to twelve, depending how one counts the protrusions of the volcanic ridge that makes up the Quirinal, Viminal and Esquiline hills).

Historians are sceptical about how many of these kings existed. The kings of Rome may have been real figures who coincidentally numbered seven, or completely fictional characters. The topic is hotly debated between 'literalist' historians, who generally accept the Roman tradition and 'hyper-criticals', who feel all Roman history before the first Punic war of 264 BCE is basically invented.

on the border by day to ride home to his wife in Rome at night. This is demonstrated by a contemporary story in which a group of noblemen, part of the army besieging the city of Ardea, had nothing to do one afternoon and 'galloped off to Rome, where they arrived as darkness was beginning to close in' (Livy 1.57.8–9).

The next century saw steady expansion, but not until 396 BCE did Rome conquer the Etruscan city of Veii, sixteen kilometres away; a city so close it is today in the suburbs of modern Rome. From this point, Rome's rise to empire truly began, yet the incentive appears to have been not victory over the Etruscans but a crushing defeat by the Gauls, probably in 387 BCE. The Gauls were an expansionist people, who had migrated over the Alps more than a century earlier. After defeating the Romans in battle they occupied the city, though Roman legend insists that the Capitoline Hill remained unconquered. The Gauls did not remain in Rome and their invasion was equally devastating to nearby cities and tribes.

The disciplined Romans, with their militaristic culture, recovered fastest. They drove off the marauding Gallic army and went on to occupy towns and territories enfeebled by invasion and sack. Unlike the Gauls, the Romans had no intention of abandoning their conquests. A generation after the Gallic sack, Rome had occupied much of Latium and was contending with the Samnite peoples for control of the prosperous cities of Capua and Cumae, almost two hundred kilometres away. By 282 BCE, Rome had defeated the Samnites and the Etruscans, who were then in league with them.

The Romans founded a number of military colonies to control the regions they had conquered. Then, to facilitate the rapid movement of their armies, they began constructing the network of roads which was eventually to bind together the Mediterranean world. Significantly, the military colonies quickly became thriving cities in their own right and so considerable numbers of 'Romans' lived their lives without ever seeing Rome.

The growing size of the Roman state attracted the interest of the much larger and predatory Hellenistic kingdoms to the east. In 280 BCE, the Greek cities of southern Italy, made uncomfortable by the power and expansionist tendencies of Rome, appealed to King Pyrrhus of Epirus for support. Much to the astonishment of the Greek world, Pyrrhus and his army of tens of thousands of pikemen were fought to a standstill by the Romans. Pyrrhus won his battles, but at the cost of a crippled army (whence comes the term 'pyrrhic victory') and he was forced to withdraw. The defeat of one of the finest generals and armies in the known world marked Rome's arrival as an international power possessing all Italy south of the River Po.

Rise to empire

> It was reported that two consular armies had been lost, that Hannibal was master of Italy ... Surely any other people would have been overwhelmed by the scale of so massive a disaster. When you compare this with other calamities ... the only similarity is that they were endured with less fortitude.
>
> Livy on the aftermath of Roman defeat at
Cannae 216 BCE

For most of the remainder of the third century BCE, Rome was locked in a protracted and draining struggle with Carthage, the city which had previously been the dominant power in the western Mediterranean. Rome fought two major wars with Carthage: the first between 264 and 241 BCE and the second between 218 and 201 BCE. The first war was fought mainly in the seas about Sicily, temporarily making Rome a naval power. With its greater resources, Rome outlasted Carthage, which was forced to sue for peace. Victory left Rome in possession of Sicily and command of the seas in the west. Both conquests were to be retained for the next seven hundred years.

The legend of Atilius Regulus

During the first war with Carthage, Regulus led a Roman invasion of Africa. The invasion was a failure and Regulus was captured by the Carthaginians. The war was a drain on Carthage's resources, so Regulus was released to bear peace terms to the Roman senate. Regulus' release was conditional on the senate actually making peace; if not, Regulus was bound by oath to return to imprisonment.

As promised, Regulus delivered the peace terms. He then argued powerfully in favour of Rome continuing the war and prosecuting it more vigorously. As promised, Regulus then went back to Carthage, knowing he would be horribly punished for his actions, as indeed he was. His bravery and dedication to the state was held as a model for later generations to follow.

In the inter-war years, Rome annexed Sardinia from Carthage. This move was partly why a leading Carthaginian family, the Barcids, came to believe that a further war with Rome was inevitable. Hastrubal Barcid was the leading Carthaginian general of the first Punic war, who, according to the later historian Polybius, passed his hatred of Rome to his son, Hannibal. Hannibal spent much of his youth in Spain where Carthage was carving out new dominions. (The name of the modern Spanish city of Cartagena comes from the Latin *Carthago Nova*, which in turn comes from the Punic *Quart-Hadasht* 'New Carthage'.) Rome also had interests in Spain and secured a passage to Iberia by taking its first province outside Italy. This was originally called Gallia Transalpina but was often referred to simply as 'the Province' (hence its modern name of Provence). With tensions rising between the Romans and Carthaginians in Spain, Hannibal attacked the city of Saguntum. This city was allied to Rome, so the attack was effectively a declaration of war. Then, without waiting for a Roman response, Hannibal attacked Italy from the north.

Cannae - Rome's greatest defeat

After two defeats by Hannibal, the Romans decided on a change of strategy. Hannibal's army was disciplined and experienced but relatively small. Therefore, Rome would crush the Carthaginians by sheer weight of numbers. Levies of Roman and Italian manpower raised almost 100,000 men, the largest army ever assembled by the Republic. Hannibal's army was around half that size although his cavalry was both more numerous and more experienced: a factor which was to prove decisive.

Rather than avoid Rome's massive army, Hannibal sought battle. He also took the unusual step of using his weaker Gallic and Spanish troops to bear the brunt of the first Roman assault. The battle began with the Carthaginians chasing off the cavalry that guarded the Roman army's flanks. When the legions then hit the front ranks of Hannibal's army, the Gauls and Spaniards gave ground but did not break.

> Once the mass of Roman troops was embedded in the body of his army, Hannibal ordered his Lybian troops to close in on the flanks. At the same time the Carthaginian cavalry hit the Romans from behind. The Romans were enveloped and packed so tightly that their greater numbers were useless. Some seventy thousand men were cut down on the Roman side for the loss of about eight thousand of Hannibal's men.
>
> This disaster destroyed the Roman army as a fighting force; overall it is estimated that one in every three contemporary adult Roman males died in the Hannibalic war.

Hannibal intended to invade by way of the Po valley. Doing this necessitated taking his army, including elephants, on an epic journey across the Alps. His arrival in Italy presented the Romans with the most severe challenge to their nascent empire since the Gallic sack of Rome in the late fourth century. In 218 BCE, Hannibal won a close battle at Trebia, then wiped out a Roman army in an ambush at Lake Trasimene in 217. Finally, Hannibal's army crushed the Romans at Cannae, in 216 BCE. Though the defeat at Cannae rocked Rome to the foundations, Rome's Italian allies mostly stayed loyal. Under Rome's 'shield' – General Quintus Fabius, also known as 'the delayer' – Rome slowly rebuilt its strength. Hannibal was contained in southern Italy while Rome dedicated its military resources to the conquest of Spain. Driven from Spain, the Carthaginian army attempted to unite with Hannibal in Italy, but was defeated. Finally, a Roman army under Scipio Africanus landed in North Africa, forcing Hannibal to leave Italy to defend Carthage. Badly outnumbered and facing a skilled and experienced general, Hannibal was defeated at Zama in 202 BCE. Carthage surrendered soon after.

Rome emerged from the conflict with increased territory in northern Italy and mastery of Spain, although the Iberian tribes disputed this for the next two centuries. Despite its war-weary populace, the senate barely paused before launching Rome into another ambitious overseas war, this time against Philip V of

Macedon. Philip had opportunistically declared war on Rome after Cannae but fighting in Greece had been desultory and Rome's Aetolian allies had borne the brunt of it. Most of the action had taken place in and about a Roman protectorate in western Greece that had been established to suppress Illyrian piracy in the Adriatic. The Romans and Macedonians had soon realised that the war was a pointless waste of resources and made peace.

Then in 201 BCE Rome launched a full-scale invasion. The ostensible reason was to free Greece from Macedonian clutches, but the more probable cause was the mistaken fear that Macedon might ally with Seleucia or Ptolemaic Egypt against Rome. Both Seleucia and Egypt vastly outmatched the Romans in manpower and financial resources. However, as the Romans proved in their war with Philip V, the quality of Rome's legions was unsurpassed. The decisive battle was fought at Cynoscephalae in 197 BCE. The Roman legions of Quinctius Flamininus soundly defeated the Macedonian phalanx. After the victory, Flamininus declared Rome content at having wrested Greece from Macedonian control and the Greek city states were left to govern themselves.

However, control of Greece was an ambition of all the Hellenic powers. With Macedon defeated, Antiochus III of Seleucia attempted to fill the power vacuum in Greece by invading from the east, despite stern warnings from the Romans to stay away. The Romans backed their warnings with military force; Antiochus was defeated at Thermopylae in 191 BCE and driven from Greece. To the Seleucid king's surprise the Romans followed up their success by attacking him in his own dominions the following year. The battle of Magnesia broke the power of the Seleucid empire which thereafter went into a slow but irreversible decline. From the Roman perspective, the wars against the Hellenistic powers were pre-emptive but defensive, so they neither followed up their victories nor expanded their empire eastward.

Even after a third war with Macedon, in which the nascent power of Philip V's successor Perseus was crushed at the battle of Pydna in 168 BCE, Rome was content not to hold territory but remain as the hegemonic power in Greece. Yet Rome was growing both more arrogant and more secure as the dominant power in the Mediterranean. The city tolerated neither the regained strength of Carthage nor the constant petty wars in Greece. When Rome defeated a Macedonian uprising by an anti-Roman king, Macedon became a Roman province. While they were about it the Romans declared war on the Achaean League, then the dominant power in Greece and crushed it in a one-sided campaign. In the same year, 146 BCE, Rome sacked and utterly destroyed Carthage and horrified the Greek world by meting out almost the same treatment to the ancient city of Corinth.

From 133 BCE, internal political strife wracked the increasingly dysfunctional political system of the Republic; but political turmoil within Rome served only to drive faster expansion. Also in 133, King Attalus of Pergamon died, leaving his rich kingdom to Rome. (Pergamon was one of the many states that had arisen from the former lands of the shrinking Seleucid Empire.) The tax revenues from their new acquisition increased Roman interest in the financial possibilities of empire. Iberia, with its silver mines, had the potential to be equally profitable but Roman misgovernment had kept the region in such disorder that the cost of suppressing repeated rebellions outweighed the gains from tax revenue.

The beginning of the first century BCE saw Rome on the defensive against a Germanic people, the Cimbri. The Cimbri were a migratory people, who had wandered northern Europe for almost a century. Allied with the Teutons and other tribes they turned southward to threaten Italy. An early attempt to head off the invasion led to a Roman army being wiped out in Gaul, but fortunately for Rome the invaders turned aside from the Alps. When the migrant tribesmen returned the Roman army was ready. It was led by Caius Marius, a demagogic politician but a dogged and skilled general who had played a pivotal role in winning Numidia from the renegade King Jugurtha a few years earlier. To win his campaign in Africa Marius had made far-reaching changes to the Roman army, which included new forms of recruitment, training and military formations. These proved highly successful in campaigns against the Germanic tribes and Marius was elected to command the army year after year.

Expansion in the age of the dynasts

> The Romans are the common enemy of mankind, most vicious where the loot is greatest. By audacity and deceit, leapfrogging from war to war, they have grown great. They will destroy humanity, or perish in the process.
>
> To the king of Parthia from the king of Pontus
> *Sallust Letter of Mithridates* 1.20

Rome's expansion to empire followed an exponential curve. Modest resources had resulted in modest gains; Rome's genius lay in assimilating those gains so comprehensively that within a few generations the people of occupied lands in Italy considered themselves Roman. With conquered peoples fully subscribed to the Roman project, the resources for further conquest were that much greater.

Who were the dynasts?

A 'dynast' in Greek is 'one who is able to do something'. This term rapidly came to mean 'able to rule', whence our modern word 'dynasty'. The 'age of the Dynasts' is often used instead of the term 'Late Republic' to reflect that after 88 BCE Rome was effectively ruled by a succession of strongmen who had near-monarchical powers.

However, these dynasts were not autocrats, because their power was bitterly disputed, both by the senate and by high-ranking families ambitious for their members to become dynasts themselves. On two occasions three dynasts banded together to rule the state as what the writer Varro called 'a three-headed monster'. The first of these 'triumvirates' was an informal pact that linked Julius Caesar, Crassus and Pompey. The second was a formally instituted quasi-constitutional office in which Lepidus, Mark Antony and Octavian divided the empire among them.

The power struggles between the dynasts and their opponents effectively destroyed what remained of the Republican constitution. When the empire was established, it was in effect a military dictatorship, yet the reaction of the common people was not outrage but relief that the political turbulence of the previous era had ended.

However, after the Punic wars Rome was sparing in granting citizenship to conquered nations and a social and legal divide grew between Romans and provincials. Consequently even as the last years of the Republic saw the borders of Rome's empire expanding chaos and civil war took root at home. By this time Rome had huge resources and an economy at least in part funded by the proceeds of conquest. Also the militaristic culture of Rome inseparably linked political success with military glory. These two forces created a dynamic that forced the Roman Republic into a final surge of conquest even as the political structure of the Republic was collapsing. The first signs of this collapse were visible by 133 when a far-sighted tribune, Tiberius Gracchus, attempted to deal with the two dominant problems facing Rome – a decline in the number of peasant farmers, who had once been the backbone of the legions and the dangerous and growing disaffection of the non-Roman peoples of Italy.

The decline in the number of Roman smallholders available for recruitment into the army was compensated by Marius' change to the rules, allowing those without significant property to join the legions. However, the selfish and short-sighted

Roman nobility did nothing about the resentment felt by the people of Italy towards Roman arrogance and injustice. The Italians appealed for Roman citizenship not from love of Rome but because Roman citizens had legal protection against abuses denied to the Italians. When proposed legislation to grant citizenship to many Italians failed (and the tribune proposing the law was murdered) in 91 BCE, the Italians responded by declaring war on Rome.

The war lasted for over two years. It was called the Social War (from the Latin *socii*, 'allies') and is perhaps the only recorded case of the opposite of a war of independence. The Italians wanted to become Roman and were prepared to destroy Rome if they were denied citizenship. The Italians had the same armour, training and tactics as the Romans, so the Social War was very close to a civil war. In effect, Rome lost that war: the senate backed down and the Roman people agreed to grant citizenship to anyone who would stop fighting them to get it. This broke the back of the rebellion, though some diehard Samnite tribes continued to fight for the total obliteration of Rome.

Even before the flames of the Social War had died out in 88 BCE, another huge war broke out in the east. Pontus, like Pergamon, was a kingdom that had grown from the ruins of the Seleucid Empire in Asia Minor. Under King Mithridates VI, Pontus had expanded to include substantial domains around the Black Sea. Pontus was immensely rich; but in their eagerness to provoke war and get those riches the corrupt and greedy Roman officials in Asia Minor forgot that Pontus was also immensely well-armed. Mithridates swept the Romans aside and went on to conquer all Asia Minor, helped by the hatred of the people there for Rome's brutal and extortionist tax gatherers. Indeed, once he had conquered Asia Minor, Mithridates ordered the execution of all Latin-speakers in his realm and the vengeful peoples of Asia Minor massacred eighty thousand Romans and Italians in a single day.

Though nearly bankrupt, Rome raised an army to confront Mithridates. Command of that army went to the consul Cornelius Sulla, but amid scenes of rioting, political chaos and near-anarchy in Rome, Caius Marius used his political allies to transfer the command to himself. As his army remained loyal, Sulla marched his men into Rome where he forcibly restored order and exiled Marius before leading the army to Greece, which Mithridates had wrested from Roman control. Sulla's action set a precedent. No Roman general had ever before turned his troops against the senate and people of the city; and previously no troops would have followed a commander who did so. However, Sulla's army included new Italian citizens who had fought against Rome only two years before. Others (thanks to the Marian reforms) had no land to retire to when they were discharged. Therefore, they looked to their commander to see that they were suitably rewarded once their period of service ended. In short, for the first time, but emphatically not the last, Rome was confronted by an army more loyal to its commander than to Rome.

After Sulla had departed for Greece to campaign against Mithridates, his enemies rapidly regained power. Marius returned to Rome and began a bloody purge of Sulla's supporters. However, he could do nothing about Sulla himself, for Roman armies were fully capable of supporting themselves in the field without money or supplies from home. Consequently, though outlawed Sulla was able to reconquer Greece, force Mithridates into submission and then lead his army of very experienced veterans to reconquer Rome in a short but vicious civil war. A young volunteer general, Gnaeus Pompey, joined forces with Sulla; while Sulla took vengeance, with interest, on Marius' supporters Pompey reclaimed Africa from Marian control. Iberia was a tougher nut to crack as the Marian general there was the highly competent Sertorius. With the help of loyal tribesmen and his own rebel Romans, Sertorius fought the legions to a standstill but once Sertorius had been assassinated, Pompey easily defeated Sertorius' subordinates.

Spartacus: freedom fighter?

In a very real sense, we do not know who Spartacus was. The name, which comes from a town in Thrace, was almost certainly the *nom de guerre* of an army deserter and bandit sentenced to die as a gladiator in Cumae.

It is certain that Spartacus was one of the greatest military tacticians in an age rich in outstanding generals. From his well-planned breakout from the slave barracks where he was housed as a gladiator, to commander of an army numbering tens of thousands, Spartacus regularly outmanoeuvred and defeated the soldiers of the world's greatest army in their home country.

Fellow gladiators made up only the core of Spartacus' army. The remainder were escaped slaves and free men from the rural poor who gleefully leapt at the opportunity of plundering the estates of the rich who occupied their land. During the three years of his rebellion Spartacus plundered Italy from bottom to top and back again. He not only won battles against hastily raised Roman levies but also against a veteran legion summoned from Gaul to defeat him.

The fact that the enslaved and dispossessed joined his army reflected the social conditions of the time rather than support for Spartacus' ideology. Spartacus was no idealist. He was happy to enslave his prisoners and to make them fight as gladiators to entertain his men. As far as can be determined, his objective was plunder on as large a scale as possible. When his army reached the Alpine passes that would have taken them to freedom in the German forests they decided instead to return to looting Italy. Whether Spartacus was forced to acquiesce as legend says is impossible to know.

Eventually the slave army was destroyed in a hard-fought battle near Brundisium. Spartacus' body was never found, but the vindictive Romans crucified thousands of captured slaves along the Appian Way as a grim warning of the consequences of rebellion.

The general who eventually defeated Spartacus was Licinius Crassus, the richest man in Rome. Crassus had ambitions in the east where Mithridates was resurgent. Among those who opposed the Pontic king's attacks on Roman Asia Minor was a young man called Julius Caesar. Caesar had been appointed to a high rank in the priesthood when Sulla's enemies ruled Rome and had barely escaped with his life when Sulla returned. He had gone east in part because he felt unsafe in Rome, which was dominated by followers of Sulla.

The power of Mithridates was eventually broken by a Roman general, Licinius Lucullus, who pursued him deep into Armenia. This brought him into conflict with the Armenian monarch Tigranes the Great and Lucullus achieved one of the greatest victories of Roman arms when his diminutive army smashed Tigranes' forces at Tigranocerta in 69 BCE. Despite his victory, Lucullus was unable to keep the loyalty of his men. The army was operating far from its home territory, without a mandate from the senate and the troops wanted to stand down. Eventually the army refused to leave its camp and Lucullus was replaced by Pompey.

Not only Mithridates but also pirates were a major threat to Rome's eastern empire in the seventies BCE. Huge fleets of pirate ships not only attacked merchant shipping but also raided towns and foraged deep into Italy. Among the many captured by their depredations was Julius Caesar. When Pompey replaced Lucullus he was at the height of his power and popularity as he had smashed the power of those pirates in a few short months. This was partly through Pompey's exceptional command of logistics and organisation, and partly because of the exceptional and unprecedented powers granted to him by the people of Rome; powers that were later to become part of the constitutional authority of Rome's emperors. Pompey organised a huge sweep of the Mediterranean, starting from the west and driving the pirates back to their bases in Cilicia and Crete, where they were besieged and defeated. Having dealt with the pirates, not only did Pompey finish off Mithridates, he also subdued much of the Middle East and conquered Jerusalem. The former domains of Mithridates were absorbed by the rapidly expanding Roman Empire.

Rome was also gaining new territory in the west. Julius Caesar became consul despite the enmity of the aristocratic faction in the senate known as the *optimates* ('best men'). The optimates were Romans who felt that their aristocratic birth and huge wealth entitled them to a leading role in Roman politics. After his consulship, thanks to the support of Crassus and Pompey, Caesar became the governor of Transalpine Gaul. His office gave him command of four legions which he used to embark on a campaign to conquer the rest of Gaul. Caesar's opportunity came when Gaul was threatened by invading Helvetian tribesmen; an invasion intended to permanently displace many Gallic tribes. These tribes gratefully accepted Roman help to repel the marauders, especially as Caesar also turned his attention to the Germanic Suebi tribe that was attempting to colonise parts of Gaul. However, Gallic gratitude soured when it became plain that once the Roman army had moved onto their land it had no intention of withdrawing. The wealth Caesar made from his victories allowed him to fight his wars in Gaul despite growing opposition and resentment in the senate in Rome. Caesar even raised his own legions without the senate's knowledge and used them to make further conquests in the area that is now Belgium. In 55 BCE Caesar led his legions across the channel to make a reconnaissance of southern Britain, a land which the Romans had until then considered a mist-shrouded land of legend.

The people of Gaul had never considered they were a single nation but faced with a de facto Roman conquest, they united in a bid for independence under the leadership of the charismatic Vercingetorix. The Gauls rose in revolt while Caesar was in Italy attempting to shore up his political defences in response to rising opposition in the senate. Caesar boldly returned across the deep snow of the Alpine passes, only to suffer a setback when he attempted to crush the rebel stronghold in Gergovia. However, even united, the Gallic people were no match for the Roman legions and Vercingetorix was trapped in the fortress town of Alesia. Attempts by the Gauls to break out failed as did a simultaneous attempt by relieving troops to break in. With the surrender of Vercingetorix Gaul became part of the Roman Empire.

Caesar conquered Gaul for personal prestige and political power rather than for strategic considerations. His conquest came at the cost of the death or enslavement of millions of Gauls. Nevertheless, once absorbed into the Roman Empire Gaul rapidly became a peaceful and productive province where Roman language law and values became so deeply embedded that they remain an essential part of modern French culture.

The dying republic

O tempora, o mores! – Oh, the times, the [lack of] morality!

Cicero condemning the debauched revolutionary
Catiline, *Against Catiline* 1.1.2

Caesar was not alone in hankering for military glory on a grand scale. Pompey, with his conquest of Asia Minor, had already achieved this and in the process replaced Crassus as the richest man in Rome. So while Caesar was adding vast domains to the empire in the west, Crassus decided to emulate Pompey in the east. By this time the Seleucid Empire was virtually extinct, replaced by the warrior peoples of Parthia who had raised an empire of their own. The Parthians kept to their side of the Euphrates – the recognised border with Rome – and stayed studiously neutral during Rome's wars with Armenia and Pontus. Crassus' invasion of Parthian lands was therefore condemned, with good reason, as blatant aggression.

Cicero - philosopher and statesman

The final years of the Republic saw some of the most iconic figures to ever walk the stage of Roman history. Pompey, Julius Caesar, Cleopatra and Cato are all deservedly remembered. However, none of these possessed the wide range of abilities of Marcus Tullius Cicero, a country boy from Arpinum, who rose to the leadership of Rome on two crucial occasions.

The first was the Catiline Conspiracy when the heavily indebted and highly aristocratic Catiline attempted to emulate Sulla and take over Rome by force. Cicero was then consul; the first of his family to rise so high. He exposed Catiline's machinations and excoriated the man in a series of speeches that survive today. At the end of his life Cicero rallied the state against Mark Antony, only to be betrayed by Octavian – later Augustus – in one of history's most spectacular double-crosses. Cicero's portrayal of Antony as a lecherous, drunken lout remains convincing, even today. When he came to power a furious Antony had Cicero executed but his image was forever stained.

Cicero was more than a statesman and orator. He was also a writer and a philosopher whose letters have given us an unprecedented, almost day-to-day, picture of life in the Late Republic. His musings on the constitution, old age and the afterlife give us an unparalleled insight into the mind of an educated Roman of the day.

Had Crassus succeeded, Rome would have gained an empire that stretched from the Atlantic to the mountains of Afghanistan, but Parthia was an attempted conquest too far. The Roman legionaries fought best against the same sort of people as themselves. Most of Rome's conquests had cities and centres of power that could easily be identified and captured. It was no coincidence that Rome's borders lay where the urban culture of the Mediterranean ended at the Atlas mountains of Africa and the forests of Germany. Although Parthia possessed cities, notably the capital of Ctesiphon in Mesopotamia, empty and arid tracts of land lay between these cities and Rome. In any case, the true power of the Parthians lay in the country estates of the non-urban aristocracy. Consequently the Romans failed to ever truly conquer Parthia and Crassus never even came close. He was nonplussed by fast-moving archers on horseback, who retreated as his heavy infantry tried to come to grips with them. Then when the legions began to waver under a storm of arrows, heavily armoured horsemen, cataphracts, charged and broke their ranks.

Crassus was killed by the Parthians at Carrhae in 53 BCE. His death broke the alliance with Pompey and Caesar that had kept Caesar's enemies in the Roman senate in check. Pompey now joined these enemies, who demanded that Caesar be prosecuted on his return from Gaul. In its eagerness to see Caesar brought down the senate acted unconstitutionally; illegal behaviour which gave Caesar an excuse to invade Italy with his veteran army. Though Caesar was eventually victorious in his civil war, he had no remedy for the problems that plagued the Republic and his attempt to rule as a dictator ended with his assassination.

The Ides of March

Caesar was of the generation which had seen parents, uncles and other relatives butchered in the strife between Sulla and Marius. He had no intention of following this path and consequently made a point of accepting the surrender of any Roman who yielded to him in the civil war. Though defeated, many of those who had surrendered were far from reconciled. The leader of this faction was a young man, Marcus Brutus, who was allegedly a descendant of the legendary Brutus who had expelled the last of the kings from Rome. The fact that Caesar had a long-standing adulterous relationship with Brutus' mother may have added to his animosity.

The conspirators struck on the Ides of March (that is, the fifteenth) when Caesar was attending the senate. Mark Antony, Caesar's supporter and a powerful fighter, was delayed outside by a ruse while the senators attacked Caesar with daggers they had concealed under their togas. When he saw he was doomed Caesar pulled his toga over his head and collapsed, ironically at the foot of a statue of his defeated foe, Pompey. His famous last words '*et tu Brute?*' (You also, Brutus?) are almost certainly a later invention.

Caesar had dismissed his bodyguard, believing that everyone knew that killing him would lead to turmoil immeasurably worse than his dictatorship. He was right about the turmoil, but underestimated the vindictiveness of his fellow senators. In fact,

Caesar's assassination plunged the empire into two further bouts of civil war. The first was between Caesar's successors – led by his henchman Mark Antony and his heir Octavian – and the faction led by Caesar's assassins, Brutus and Cassius. Antony and Octavian were allied with the Caesarian general, Lepidus. The three formed a body known as the second triumvirate which ruthlessly purged Italy of enemies, real or imagined. Sometimes men were purged less for political offences than simply to seize wealth with which to pay the triumvirate's supporters. Caesar's assassins had fled to the east where Caesar's death was ultimately avenged at Philippi in Greece in a battle in which both Brutus and Cassius died.

After Philippi, Lepidus was pushed aside and Octavian commanded most of the western empire, while Antony took charge of the east. The economy of the west had been badly damaged by previous rounds of civil wars while the eastern provinces were richer and more populous. Antony intended to cover himself in glory in a Parthian campaign to avenge Crassus. Then he could turn on Octavian who would by then have become deeply unpopular in his attempts to salvage the ruined fortunes of Italy.

Cleopatra

Despite the modern misconceptions, Cleopatra was not particularly African. She was a Macedonian Greek, and more pure-bred than most, since her immediate family had practised brother–sister marriage from the time that her ancestor Ptolemy (one of the generals of Alexander the Great) had seized control of Egypt in 323 BCE.

In 47 BCE, Cleopatra used the support of Caesar to gain power in a dynastic struggle and thereafter was dependent on Rome for her political survival. At the time of Caesar's assassination she had moved to Rome with her (and Caesar's) son to put political pressure on the dictator.

Once Antony became triumvir and ruler of the east Cleopatra had little choice but to throw in her lot with his. This she did with considerable flair and enthusiasm, for she and Antony had characters so highly compatible that they had several children together, despite the fact that Antony had married Octavian's sister in an attempt to bring the triumvirate closer.

Octavian used the betrayal of his sister to portray Antony as a drunken sot bewitched by the decadent oriental wiles of Cleopatra, even though Cleopatra seems to have been a conscientious and hard-working monarch whose main political ambition was to remain loyal to Rome at all costs.

When Octavian declared war on Cleopatra and defeated her and Antony, the pair fled to Egypt where they spent their last days in a round of frantic partying. On news of Octavian's arrival in Egypt Antony killed himself. Cleopatra was imprisoned; but believing she was being kept alive only to decorate Octavian's coming triumphal parade in Rome, she arranged for a venomous snake to be smuggled to her and died from its bite.

Antony miscalculated. Octavian turned out to be a genius at political manoeuvring and superb in his choice of subordinates to carry the burden of restoring the west. When Antony's campaign in Parthia failed ignominiously, Octavian turned on him. More precisely Octavian turned on Cleopatra, knowing that if he declared war on Egypt Antony would have to support his ally. Octavian's choice of enemy had a further benefit, for when Cleopatra and Antony were defeated in a naval battle at Actium in Greece, not only the eastern Roman Empire but also Egypt fell into his hands.

Thus by the end of 31 BCE power over Rome and its empire was concentrated in the hands of a single individual. Others had been in this position before, but never had Rome's domains been so vast, nor the institutions of the empire so ripe for reform. Octavian began playing down his identity as the son of Julius Caesar (he seldom used his modern appellation of Octavian, preferring to call himself 'Caesar' from the start). He allowed the senate to award him the name Augustus ('the revered one') and began the slow process of changing his image from conquering warlord to constitutional ruler. As Augustus, he began the task of melding Rome's diverse imperial possessions into a unified empire; a task that was to continue for centuries.

The peoples of the empire

> Caelia, you give yourself to Germans, you won't stay out of the beds of Cilicians and Cappadocians, you have an Egyptian stud ... and circumcised Jews.
>
> The poet Martial to a lady with cosmopolitan tastes
> *Epigrams* 7.30

At the end of the Republic, most 'Roman' subjects continued to live as they had before their absorption into the empire. Most peoples of the empire were not Roman citizens; many had seldom met a Roman. A good example is found in the Gospels, a near-contemporary text describing events within the empire in which Romans hardly appear at all until Pontius Pilate. The main imposition of Roman rule was financial, in that Rome demanded taxes from subject peoples (as narrated at the beginning of the Gospel of Luke). In return the Romans did their best to give value for money by enforcing peace on conquered lands, not least because warfare and unrest made the collection of taxes more difficult.

Civus Romanus sum

'I am a Roman citizen.' Uttering this proud declaration afforded the speaker a number of rights and privileges – and the death sentence if the declaration was proven to be untrue. In the ancient world, citizenship was determined by ancestry rather than current location. This was particularly true of those who were citizens of Rome. Many of these citizens were scattered among the subject peoples of the empire, who although ruled by Rome remained subjects of whatever state they had been ruled by when that state was conquered.

Subject peoples paid taxes and were subject to a provincial governor but were not Romans. Romans might live in the provinces in groups, such as when colonies of legionary veterans were retired en masse to create a new city, or as individuals who were favoured with the grant of Roman citizenship in return for services rendered to the Roman state. Thus, a Cilician maker of tents for the Roman army, Saul of Tarsus was a Roman citizen. Later, as Paul the apostle, he used his citizen's rights to bypass the edicts of a provincial governor and demand that his case be heard in Rome.

In keeping with its status as an urban civilisation, the city-state (*civitas*) was the basic unit of Roman administration. (The word 'civilisation' is derived from *civitas*.) Every Roman province was a mosaic of such city-states, each with its surrounding territory of agrarian land. Where the necessary urban centres did not exist, the Romans created them, thus providing an impetus towards urbanisation and Romanisation in areas unfamiliar with either concept. However where cities already existed the Romans generally kept government and administration in local hands, though with a preference towards government by oligarchies of local aristocrats rather than for Greek-style democracy. This is not to say that democracy did not exist under Roman rule but rather that such democracy was of the Roman style, where voters selected which local aristocrats they preferred to run their *civitas*. Non-aristocrats need not apply for elections and of course, the autocratic government in Rome could overrule local statutes whenever it felt the need; but within these constraints democracy flourished.

When the Romans founded a town they gave it a constitution. An excellent example comes from Colonia Genetiva Iulia Urbanorum (in southern Spain). This constitution was written on bronze tablets discovered almost intact in 1870. The people of 'colonies' such as this were constitutionally Romans rather than natives; indeed many colonists were retired soldiers established on the land as a way of securing the area. This policy began at an early date and continued through the Republican empire. Colonies, whether in Italy or abroad, were part of the *ager Romanus*, those parts of the empire which were directly owned and administered by Romans. Technically speaking all other lands remained the property of separate, subject peoples, whom the Romans usually ruled indirectly through those people's customary administrative machinery. Some states, such as Rhodes in the Mediterranean, joined Rome as allies (*civitates foederatae*). Theoretically allies were free and independent under the Roman hegemony. They included many of the cities of Italy, where we begin this brief survey of the empire at the end of the Republican era.

Italy

Another generation has been pulverised by civil war
And Rome has ruined herself with her own power.

Horace, *Epode* 16.1–2 on the destruction of Italy by
warring Roman armies

Until the time of Augustus, Italy was a purely geographical description. All that its peoples had in common was that they had suffered brutally in the civil wars. There was no common language, law, ethnicity or culture. In the north, the population was Gallic. The city of Mediolanum (Milan), captured by the Romans from the Celtic Insubres in 222 BCE was the provincial capital of what the Romans called Cisalpine Gaul: 'Gaul on this side (of the Alps)'. Even today, one can see how the chaotic street patterns of the Gallic city centre give way to regular blocks of houses as the city expanded along Roman lines. This provides a good metaphor for the Roman occupation, where Roman culture gradually overlaid the original Gallic. Outside the cities, Roman roads such as the Via Aemilia were efficiently policed, which allowed people and trade to move freely and bring new ideas along with new materials. Nevertheless even at the end of the Republican era not all of northern Italy had been subdued by Rome. Hard fighting with mountain tribes was still to come.

In central Italy Rome's was one of several competing cultures. The Etruscans to the north had largely been assimilated by Rome; two generations on, the emperor Claudius would study Etruscan as a dead language. However the Samnites of the mountains remained proudly nationalistic, even under Roman domination, and in the south the inhabitants of cities such as Neapolis and Tarentum thought of themselves as Greek. (Indeed, even in the twenty-first century the people of some southern Italian towns still speak Greek.) Roman citizenship had become widespread after the Social War of 90 BCE and became even more common later, as politicians such as Caesar enfranchised entire regions in order to garner their votes. Yet still many Italians were not Romans nor even very favourably inclined towards Rome. 'Roman Italy' was a work in progress.

Greece

Greece has conquered her crude conqueror.

The poet Horace on the spread of Greek culture
Epistles 2.1.156

In Greece many persisted in regarding the Romans as occupying barbarians. Corinth had still not recovered from the devastation of 146 BCE. More recently, in 86 BCE, Sulla had stormed Athens with such violence that blood ran down the gutters through the city gates. Consequently Roman culture had not made much headway in Greece, though the reverse was not true.

Since the time of Scipio Africanus, aristocratic Romans had become increasingly Hellenophilic. By the end of the Republic most senators were bilingual in Greek and Latin and were familiar with Homeric verse. Greek sculpture, art, medicine and philosophy were considered superior to the Roman counterparts that they largely replaced. It became common for aristocratic youths of the last generation of the Roman Republic to tour Greece – a friend of Cicero's spent so much time there that he acquired the nickname 'Atticus' (from 'Attica', the region of Greece in which Athens is situated). By the end of the Republic the process of fusion which was to create a Graeco-Roman culture was well under way. This was seen very clearly in the merging (syncretism) of Greek and Roman religious beliefs, in which Roman gods assimilated most of the characteristics of their Greek equivalents while retaining their Roman names; for example Juno for the Greek Hera, Mercury for Hermes and so on. Militarily, Rome had unfinished business in the lands which today make up Albania and the Balkans. These were to remain outside the empire for another generation.

Divine aliases - Roman and Greek gods in syncresis		
Roman	Greek	
Jupiter	Zeus	king of the gods
Juno	Hera	queen of the gods
Pluto	Hades	lord of the underworld
Neptune	Poseidon	ruler of the sea
Minerva	Athena	goddess of wisdom
Diana	Artemis	goddess of the hunt
Apollo	Apollo	god of the arts (including prophecy)
Bacchus	Dionysus	god of wine
Mercury	Hermes	god of boundaries, messenger of Zeus
Hercules	Heracles	superhero who became a god
Mars	Ares	god of war
Vulcan	Hephaestus	craftsman god
Venus	Aphrodite	goddess of love

Asia Minor

> Romans, the revenues of the other provinces are such that we
> scarcely derive enough income from them to pay for their own
> protection but Asia is rich and productive...
>
> Cicero, *For the Manilian Law* 14

Under the Republic the Romans were heartily hated in Asia
Minor. The Seleucids and their successors in Asia Minor had
developed a strong fusion of Hellenic and native cultures while
Rome was a brutal and alien presence. After the Mithridatic
wars, Asia Minor was comprehensively looted by its Roman
conquerors. Governors imposed high taxes and swingeing fines
on the cities and once the municipalities were indebted they
were forced to take out loans too large to repay, and then driven
further into bankruptcy by compound interest on their debts.
By the start of the imperial era a measurable fraction of the
population of Asia Minor had been sold into slavery and trans-
ported to Italy. These slaves were much in demand as teachers,
doctors and clerks (the son of the last king of Macedon ended
his days as a lawyer's clerk). Many of these slaves later earned
their freedom and contributed to the combined Graeco-
Roman culture of the empire.

Beyond the Hellenistic culture of the cities the peoples of
the interior of Asia Minor lived very different lives depending
on their locations in the extremely fractured geography of the
region. There were Gauls living on the arid central plateau –
the same Galatians to whom St Paul wrote his famous letter –
and there were worshippers of the Persian Ahura-Mazda in the
mountains of the east. So difficult and impenetrable were many
of the interior fastnesses of Anatolia that not only did Roman
rule sit lightly, it is probable that many of the common people
were unaware that they were Roman subjects at all.

Iberia

> Pompey [the younger] was able to draw out the war because
> that country was full of mountains and extremely well adapted
> to defence. Though it has extremely fertile soil and abundant
> springs, nevertheless it is very difficult to get around.
>
> Caesar's Spanish War 8

Though dominated by Rome for the last century of the Republic, Iberia had rarely been peaceful. The Celtiberians and Lusi-
tanians chafed under Roman rule that was seldom benevolent.
Even when the native people were not up in arms on their
own behalf, the peninsula was a battleground between warring
factions of the dysfunctional and dying Republic. While there
were Roman armies in Hispania as early as 216 BCE, every
generation of Romans since had fought there. Julius Caesar did
so twice, once fighting Spanish tribesmen and quashing the sons
of his rival Pompey. Two legions, the Sixth and Seventh, were
quartered in Hispania for so long that the camp became a city,
today called Leon (from Legion).

Carthaginian influence on Iberia had largely been eradi-
cated but Roman culture was limited to the eastern coast with
a considerable push for urbanisation in the north-west, where
– among others – the towns of Asturica Augusta (Astorga) and
Caesarea Augusta (Zaragosa) were soon to be founded. For
most of the tribes of the interior, life under Roman rule was
little different from that of previous generations. At this time
Hispania was roughly divided into two administrative areas:
Nearer Spain and Further Spain. Further reorganisation would
take place under Augustus, but at the start of the imperial era
few of the resentful and oppressed peoples of the peninsula
could have foreseen the centuries of peace and prosperity that
lay ahead.

Gaul

War and tyrants were always in Gaul until you submitted to our authority.

Roman general Petellius Cerialis addresses rebellious
Gauls in Tacitus. *Histories* 4.74

Though spared the ravages suffered by Greece, Africa and other provinces that hosted the warring armies of Rome's civil wars, Gaul too entered the imperial era in a battered condition thanks to the brutality of Caesar's conquest. In the years immediately preceding Caesar's arrival, Gaul had been developing along lines strongly affected by Mediterranean culture. Urbanism and coinage had spread and the nascent Gallic sense of nationhood was first forced into rapid growth and then crushed by the Roman invaders. Rome took the existing tribal cantons as the basis of civil administration, making sixty-five of them into *civitates*, with the intention of turning the principal town of each into a proper Roman city. The usually tolerant Romans objected strongly to the practices of Druidism and stamped them out whenever possible. In consequence, though most Gauls continued to worship their own gods the process of syncretism had already begun: the god Lugus was identified with Mercury, Taranis with Jupiter and so on.

The end of the first century BCE saw Gaul in the process of recovering from the economic and demographic devastation of the previous half-century. Outside the Romanised southern province of Gallia Transalpina – renamed Narbonensis – the Roman presence was mainly limited to soldiers on the frontiers and merchants and administrators in the towns. Nevertheless Roman influence was noticeable everywhere for the chilling effect it had on the inter-tribal wars which had blighted pre-conquest life. Like Iberia, Gaul was set for centuries of peace which would ineradicably embed a Gallic form of Roman culture into the region. But also like Iberia, few appreciated this at this time.

Africa

> *Ex Africa semper aliquid novi.* (There's always something new out of Africa.)
>
> Pliny the Elder, *Natural History* 8.42

If Africa would provide marvels to Pliny's generation, to the earlier Romans of the Republic it was almost another world. Its elephants, monkeys, leopards and other fauna surprised and amazed the Romans, who traded rumours of even stranger creatures and peoples dwelling deep in the continent's interior. Just as 'Asia' to the Romans meant the province formerly known as Pergamon in Anatolia, 'Africa' (properly 'Africa Proconsularis') meant the former domains of Carthage which had been appended to the annexed kingdom of Numidia to make a new province. Africa was divided into the coastal plains north of the Atlas mountains and the deserts of the interior. The settled coastal region had been known to the Italians for centuries; its figs and corn were familiar and welcome produce in the markets of Italy. The wild interior of the province was almost unknown territory, whose nomadic tribes such as the Garamantes were yet to be convinced that they lived under Roman jurisdiction.

Egypt

> Her monstrous gods of every form and barking Anubis, are opposed to Neptune, Venus and Minerva.
>
> Virgil on the defeat of Cleopatra, *Aeneid* 8.698–700

Egypt joined the Roman Empire as the imperial era began. From the beginning Egypt was an exceptional province. Octavian, who acquired Egypt from the defeated Cleopatra in 30 BCE, treated the country as a personal possession rather than as an integral part of the Roman Empire. Later, as Octavian evolved into Augustus, his propaganda depicted him to the Egyptians as a pharaoh *in absentia.* Egypt was governed not by a proconsul or legate, as was customary elsewhere, but by an Equestrian prefect serving as the emperor's personal representative (see below for Equestrians and other ranks in the empire). Senators were forbidden to enter Egypt without permission. Egypt was, and was to remain, an imperial anomaly. This perception has been strengthened in modern times because the nature of the evidence from Roman Egypt is different from the rest of the empire. The desert sands have preserved a wealth of information on papyrus that is simply not available from wetter climes. Through letters, petitions and family records we know a lot more about the everyday lives of Egyptians than we do of, for example, contemporary Gauls.

Augustus simply inserted himself into the ruling position in Egypt and left the underlying structures of Ptolemaic rule intact. Since the Ptolemies had done roughly the same with the Pharaohs they had supplanted (via a Persian governor or two), most Egyptians continued to live as their ancestors had done. They worshipped their pantheon of gods and their lives were dictated by the annual inundation of the Nile. The exception in an exceptional state was the Ptolemaic capital of Alexandria. This was an outward-looking city with a Mediterranean culture and a population made up of Egyptians, Greeks and Jews that required the presence of an entire legion (III Cyrenaica) to keep the rival ethnic groups from each other's throats.

Client kingdoms

Rex Sociusque et Amicus. (An allied king and a friend)

Standard Roman description for a client king

The Roman empire of the Republic was held by the Roman army. This army operated on an economic principle today called 'the projection of force'. That is to say, Rome lightly garrisoned the provinces and made little attempt to secure the empire's borders. Instead the legions were positioned at locations from where they could march against a variety of threats, should these materialise. A single strategically-positioned legion, such as the Twelfth stationed in Syria could simultaneously garrison a province, oversee a troubled neighbouring kingdom (Judea) and be part of a strategic reserve against threats beyond the border (in this case, Parthia). Rather than have forces available to cope with all threats to security, the Roman army relied on instilling in potential enemies such a deep respect for what it could do that force seldom had to be applied.

Consequently some kingdoms not officially under Roman rule were so dominated by the presence of nearby Roman legions that they retained only nominal independence. Their kings came to power and ruled under Roman sufferance and in return looked to Rome for their security. Today these are called 'client kingdoms' in recognition of their dependence on Roman patronage, though the Romans themselves used the politer designation of 'friends and allies'. Client kings did not pay taxes but might be asked for contributions of money or manpower as required. Perhaps the most notorious of the client kings at the start of the imperial era was King Herod of Judea, but Rome had many other such dependants, including kings from Asia Minor to Mauretania and even (thanks to the excursion by Julius Caesar) in Britain. The most contentious of these client kingdoms was Armenia, which the Parthians also claimed to rule by proxy. Over the coming century, the question of which rival empire was to be suzerain of the mountain kingdom would be a source of considerable tension.

Friends, Romans and countrymen

In a case where a [Greek] man was accused of [pretending to have Roman] citizenship ... the emperor made him wear a Greek cloak while being accused and a toga while being defended.

Suetonius, *Life of Claudius* 15.2

Rome's culture was exceptional in that it was openly inclusive. As the emperor Claudius noted, previous city-states such as Athens had not become greater because they strictly limited citizenship to those of their own blood. The Romans were from the start something of a mongrel people. Their foundation legend openly admitted that their main criterion for citizenship was that the claimant should have two legs and a pulse. When neither runaway slaves nor reformed bandits had been turned away, it was difficult for later Romans to claim superior birth. Some aristocrats did, notoriously the Julii, who claimed descent from Venus, but it was commonly believed that another equally aristocratic family, the Metelli, took their name from a discharged mercenary.

Regal and early Republican Rome made a habit not only of co-opting recently conquered peoples into the citizen body but sometimes (as with, for instance, Alba Longa), destroying the original city and relocating the new citizens to Rome. In some cases it was recognised that a nation that had been a bitter enemy might take time to settle into its new role as Roman. In such cases citizenship was *sine suffragio*; that is, the new Romans could not vote. Many Latin city-states were absorbed in this manner, though the policy was largely abandoned after the Punic Wars of 263–202 BCE possibly because Romans were already becoming jealous of the rights of citizenship and more wary of those to whom they granted it.

When the policy of inducting large populations into the empire began again, the new Romans were generally accepted *optimo iure* ('with the vote'), not least because the desire for their votes was the main reason why certain opportunistic politicians inducted them in the first place. Although entire cities and tribes collectively joined the Roman citizen body, citizenship was also highly attainable by individuals. Rome was unique in allowing private individuals to create new citizens by means other than childbearing. This was because, once freed, slaves became both citizens and junior members of their former master's house-hold. Manumission was very common; slaves might be freed in their ex-master's will or while the master was still alive, either from gratitude for services rendered or from simple friendship. Tiro, the friend and former slave of Cicero, is a good example. Two groups that particularly benefited from manumission were Greeks and Asians, whose higher degree of education allowed them privileged roles in upper-class Roman households, and a third group were Jews whose co-religionists banded together to buy them from slavery.

For those peoples and tribes to whom they did not grant citizenship, the Romans often gave Latin Rights, by which favoured communities had privileges such as the right to trade in Roman markets (the *ius commercio*) and the right to marry Roman citizens (*conubium*). In these circumstances the child of a Roman father was also Roman, or if the father had Latin rights the child inherited them. Finally, early in the imperial era, service as an auxiliary in the Roman army resulted in the soldier receiving citizenship after a full term of service and an honourable discharge. Even in the later Republic, the importance of citizenship lay not in the vote, for voting had to be done in person in Rome and many 'Romans' lived hundreds of miles away. More important was the universal protection of Roman law. (It was counted against the later emperor Galba that he had executed a man who had claimed to be a Roman citizen, but even Galba crucified his victim on a higher and better cross than condemned provincials.)

One consequence of the Roman approach to citizenship was the suppression of nationalist sentiments. These were limited in any case, as most peoples of the empire were loyal firstly to their immediate community and tribe rather than their wider national group. Parochial loyalties were strengthened by the fact that any given area might include towns of Roman citizens (*colonia*), several *municipia* with privileges short of full citizenship and towns with no elevated status. Yet even within such towns there was an upper class of people who either had citizenship or a realistic chance of attaining it, and others with Latin Rights. Communities within a province were more likely to consider neighbouring cities as rivals for imperial favour than as fellow nationals ground down by foreign oppression.

The fact that all races, ethnic groups and social classes could aspire to Roman citizenship mitigated their resentment of Roman rule. The unequal distribution of the privileges that citizen rights bestowed prevented the growth of a common anti-Roman sentiment, as those with such privileges rarely found common cause with those who lacked them. In the imperial era, Roman citizenship was a major force in the unification of the empire.

How the empire was governed

> Romans, never forget what you do best. Government is your art, to train men in the habit of peace; with generosity to the conquered and firmness with the insolent.
>
> The poet Vergil early in the imperial era
> *Aeneid* 6.851–3

Huge obstacles made centralised government of the Roman empire impracticable. No one is sure how large its population was at the start of the imperial era but estimates for Italy alone range from six to thirteen million people. The best – but still extremely rough – approximation of the population of the empire as a whole is somewhere between eighteen and forty million. There were considerable differences in climate, religion, culture, geography and economic circumstances in the different parts of the empire. Therefore legislation suitable for Spanish tribesmen (for example), might be irrelevant or inappropriate for Egyptians living on the second cataract of the Nile. A government that failed to take account of the local situation in each part of the empire was doomed to failure.

Administrative units from small to large

Vicus – a village, usually ruled by a headman chosen in whatever manner was traditional (whence our modern English word 'vicar')

Oppidum – a town under the administration of a nearby city

Municipium – a city with (usually) an elected governing body and rule over local *vici* and *oppida*

Colonia – a city of Roman citizens, with the rights and duties thereof

Provincia – governed by an ex-magistrate of Rome, this administrative unit included dozens of *municipia*

Throughout the history of the Roman Empire, the vast majority of citizens lived in *vici* and made their living from the land. The imperial court and the population of the great cities made up only a small percentage of the overall population. It is worth remembering that many 'events' in Roman history were significant only to the tiny proportion of citizens that made up the educated urban elite.

Rome also lacked anything resembling a modern bureaucracy. The concept of bureaucracy remained to be invented; very few people were what we would today describe as civil servants. Almost everyone directly employed by the Roman state was in the army. Furthermore, the cost of maintaining that army meant that the state had very little surplus to support an administrative infrastructure. Consequently, the entire Republican empire was run by fewer individuals than would be considered adequate for a modestly sized modern British city.

A further obstacle to central government was the physical extent of the empire in an age when overland communications could move no faster than a horse. The *mare clusum*, 'closed sea', was the period between 12 November and 10 March when winter storms made sea travel virtually impossible. This meant that a journey that took weeks via the Mediterranean instead took months of overland travel. Rome eventually set up a series of imperial post houses (*cursus publicus*) which allowed relays of messengers to carry urgent communications across the empire; a communication system copied from ancient Persia that would later be imitated by America's Pony Express. However, the sheer cost of maintaining this system ensured that it was used for only limited, high-priority traffic.

Aside from the issue of getting decrees to the scattered peoples of the empire, there was the further problem of communicating the decrees once they arrived. The population was largely illiterate and mostly dispersed in rural communities where most people kept up to date by word of mouth. These constraints forced Roman government to take the shape it did, for the only form of government possible for Rome's dominions was a devolved one: executive power had to be vested in those on the spot. Given the paucity of administrative funds, those executive positions were ideally either self-financing or held by those capable of paying their own expenses.

Local government

> Amandio and his friends urge you to vote Gnaeus Helvius Sabinus as *aedile*. He is a candidate worthy of being in our government.
>
> > Municipal election graffito scratched on to a wall
> > in Pompeii, *CIL* 4.7213

Devolved government meant that the lowest tier of Roman government, the city council of each *civitas,* was the level at which most people interacted with the state. As we have seen the form of this government varied widely from region to region, but it was most developed in Roman, Greek and Italian cities. Many of these cities enjoyed a lively public life. High positions in the city executive were eagerly sought because of the contacts and prestige they brought the holder. Both Italy and the Hellenistic world had a concept, today called *euergetism*, by which those of high social rank had to repay with good works the trust of those who had elected them. This was not charity as such, more a moral and social obligation.

In Rome, the *aediles*, which were charged with the maintenance of the city and the staging of public games, were expected to contribute towards the expenses of their office from their private funds. The cost of public buildings was often underwritten in this manner; numerous inscriptions survive in which the official charged with the building proudly points out his personal financial contribution. And although women could not hold public office they could – and energetically did – promote their families through public works. For example, Eumachia of Pompeii paid for the construction of a public building that she dedicated in the name of her son Marcus Numistrus Fronto, presumably to further his political career.

Provincial government

> While Verres was governor of Sicily the people had no redress to their own laws, senatorial decrees, or the rights any human is entitled to. All the people have left is what this greedy, lecherous swine either overlooked or was already sated with.
>
> Cicero on the governorship of Verres, *Against Verres* 1.13

By the end of the Republican era, Rome had absorbed entire geographical regions into the empire. There was a well-established machinery for the process. When the conquering general was sure his province was subdued, he informed Rome. (*Provincia* originally described not an administrative area of the empire but the area of operations of the general who fought there. *Provincia* has its origin in the words 'for conquering'.) Once the conquest had been accomplished, the senate decided if it wanted to incorporate these new gains into the empire. This was not automatic: sometimes the cost of garrisoning an area was less than the return in taxes or security. The senate twice declined to make Macedon a province after conquering the kingdom and only absorbed it after a third war, in 148 BCE. If it were decided that Rome would take over government, a commission (usually of ten senators) was dispatched to formulate the guiding principles of a constitution for the new addition to the empire.

These principles were embedded in a *Lex Provinciae*, a set of laws adopted and modified by successive governors. Much of the *lex* was to do with the status of each *civitas* in the province, usually dictated by how the local people had conducted themselves in the process of being conquered. Those who had resisted most strongly or had the misfortune to occupy a strategic area would be displaced by a Roman colony. Towns that sided with the Romans might hope to become *civitates liberae*: cities exempt from imperial taxes, some actions of provincial government, and the obligation to quarter Roman forces. In Republican times a province was governed by a consul, an ex-consul, or if one were not available, a serving or former praetor. The consuls were mainly occupied with the business of conquest, while their predecessors, now called 'proconsuls', administered the lands already conquered. The governors' term of office was a year, though some were extended (prorogued).

Because governors were largely unsupervised, abuses of power were common. One governor famously remarked that half of a term of office should be spent enriching oneself and the profits from the other half set aside to bribe the jury in the inevitable lawsuits that followed. The many nefarious ways in which a provincial governor could loot a province are described in loving detail in the orator Cicero's *Against Verres*. This is a record of the famous prosecution of Verres, the former governor of

The Gospels and the tax collectors

Two men went up into the temple to pray. One was a Pharisee and the other a tax collector. The Pharisee stood by himself and his prayer was as follows: 'Thank you God for not making me like other men, extortionists, unjust, adulterers, or even this tax collector. I fast twice a week; I give tithes of all that I get.' But the tax collector stood apart and would not even lift up his eyes to heaven but beat his breast, saying, 'God, be merciful to me, a sinner!

Luke 18.10–13

And as Jesus was at table in the house, behold, many tax collectors and sinners came and joined with Jesus and his disciples in their meal. When the Pharisees saw this, they complained to the disciples, 'Why does your rabbi eat with tax collectors and sinners?' But when he [Jesus] heard them, he replied, 'It is not those who are well who need a physician but those who are sick.'

Matthew 9.10–12

When the tax collectors came to be baptised, they said to him 'Master, what shall we do?' He told them 'Collect no more than you are authorised to do.'

Luke 3.12–13

As soon as they arrived in Capernaum, the collectors of the two-drachma tax hurried to Peter and said 'Does your master not pay the tax?' and Peter said 'He does.'

Matthew 17.24–25

Sicily. Verres' money-making malpractices included the levying of arbitrary fines, inflicting punishments from which the victim could purchase relief, and downright looting of any valuables that caught his fancy. There were also more elaborate schemes, such as an order that taxes paid in kind (such as grain) had to be delivered to the opposite side of the island unless an exemption were purchased.

In the east, taxes were gathered by the *publicani*; companies of tax gatherers who paid the government the taxes assessed for a province and afterwards obtained that money (plus profit) from the provincials. A corrupt governor was happy – in exchange for a cut of the profits – to allow the *publicani* to collect far more than the amount to which they were entitled. It was dangerous even for Roman officials to oppose the *publicani*, who had influential connections in Rome. When in 92 BCE the legate Rutilius Rufus attempted to rein in the tax collectors in his province he was charged with committing the very extortion he had prevented and was found guilty by a corrupt jury.

Central government

SPQR (*Senatus Populusque Romae*. 'The Senate and the People of Rome'.)

> Motto carried on the banners of the Roman army
> still found on drain covers in Rome today

In theory, Republican Rome was a democracy governed by the people. The people elected their executive officers and kept them in check by two means. First was the principle of collegiality: at least two executives were elected to any post. (One possible origin of the word 'consul' is *con-sules* – two oxen yoked together at the plough.) Each official had the power to veto the other's decisions. Second, Rome had tribunes, who had the specific brief of curbing the executive and held far-reaching powers with which to do it. This was most spectacularly demonstrated by the reformist Gracchus brothers, who were grandsons of Scipio Africanus, the conqueror of Hannibal. Each brother held the tribunate in the last part of the second century. The elder brother Tiberius used his power to break a legislative deadlock by bringing Rome to a standstill; the younger brother Gaius was briefly so powerful that he was almost the ruler of Rome.

The fate of Tiberius Gracchus and his brother Gaius proved that, while Rome was technically a democracy, the organs of state had been captured by a clique of powerful aristocrats. The brothers acted within the constitution, although they pushed the

Roman magistrates

Roman magistrates were senators, drawn from a body that varied from under 300 to over 600; the numbers increased in times of political chaos, as the dynasts elevated their supporters, and decreased in times of stability when undeserving members or those from losing factions were pruned from the roster. The advent of the principate did not change the offices of the Roman magistracy though the roles of the magistrates evolved to adjust to the new system.

Quaestors

Election (in the Republic) or later appointment (by the emperor or senate) as quaestor qualified a man for admission to the senate. A quaestor was a junior magistrate who generally managed financial affairs either for a provincial governor or within Rome. (For example, the younger Cato's first magistracy was as quaestor with the treasury in Rome.)

Tribunes of the plebs

Their role as protectors of the people against overbearing aristocrats gave tribunes wide powers, though these were only effective within the boundaries of the city of Rome. A tribune could call assemblies to make laws and could also veto laws he disliked. His person was sacrosanct, so interference with a tribune in the course of his duties was not only illegal but sacrilege. Unsurprisingly, such wide powers were seen as very useful by emperors, who ensured that they received *tribunica potestas* (tribunic powers) under the 'constitution' of the principate.

Aediles

As the name suggests (*aedes* means 'building') the aediles were involved with the physical fabric of the city of Rome. The aediles oversaw the licensing of taverns and brothels and the destruction of unsafe buildings. Another function of the aediles was the arranging of state festivals and games. For these events, aediles were expected to add a substantial contribution from their own funds to the money provided by the state.

Praetor

Originally designed as a non-specific role to make up for the fact that two consuls could not be everywhere in Rome's growing empire, the praetorship rapidly developed a number of specific aspects; for example, the Praetor Perigrinus had foreigners living in

Rome as his particular responsibility. Praetors could also command armies in the absence of a consul. In later years, praetors became responsible for judging legal cases. This legal role continued in Italy in a much diminished form until the office was abolished in 1998 CE.

Consuls

The consulate was the chief executive office of the Roman Republic. Consuls were above all war leaders, but were also expected to play a role in civil legislation. As with all Republican offices the consulship operated on a collegiate principle. Rome had two consuls each with the power to veto the other's actions. When consular armies were combined, the consuls took command on alternate days. Ex-consuls were a major source of high officials for imperial government, and many consuls later went on to govern provinces. Such was the need for imperial administrators that it became customary in the Principate for each consul to resign during his year in office, to allow a successor also to hold the office.

Censor

The censors were responsible for maintaining the roll of Roman citizens, for licensing contractors to carry out public works and for the maintenance of public morality. This magistracy was not held annually but when a *lustrum* was required to count the number of Roman citizens. (Whence the modern word 'census'.) The office was generally considered one of the highest honours the state could bestow and consequently quickly became monopolised by the emperors.

legal definition of their powers to the limit, defying both the Roman senate and the reactionary oligarchs who dominated it. Consequently the brothers were effectively lynched by reactionary senators even though technically the senate played only a minor role in the official Roman constitution.

Legally speaking, the senate was a consultative body which had once advised the kings of Rome and now 'advised' the Roman people. In theory the senate neither proposed legislation nor passed laws. In practice the senate met to discuss laws and senatorial opinions (*senatus consulta*) tended to be briskly rubber-stamped into statute by compliant legislative assemblies.

The strength of the senate was that it was composed of the most powerful men in Rome. Such men had *auctoritas*, a social concept meaning they were respected for their power to get things done. How those things were done was not something the average Roman could question too closely, for Rome had no police force and an appeal to the judiciary usually ended up being decided by another senator. Violence and extortion by the powerful was a way of life. Even the tribunate, originally conceived as the protector of the people from the senate, was captured by powerful families; few of the influential tribunes of the later years of the Republic were anything but aristocrats.

The Late Republican senate had a monopoly on high office in Rome, in that all but quaestors, the lowest rank of magistrate, were sitting members of the senate. In any case, election to the quaestorship automatically conferred senatorial rank. The senate provided Rome with its provincial governors and its army commanders. It also selected where those army commanders and governors would serve (though in rare cases popular assemblies could overrule this). Furthermore the assemblies might elect officials and pass laws, but foreign policy, for anything up to a declaration of war, was traditionally a senatorial preserve. It would not be a great exaggeration to say that the provinces of the empire were controlled by Rome and Rome was controlled by the senate.

The problem for the Roman Empire was that in the last years of the Republic the senate was dysfunctional. Exactly what caused the social breakdown of the senate and the collapse of the systems of Republican government has been hotly debated. However, the most frequently offered explanation – that Rome's republic was unable to cope with the strain of empire – is almost certainly too facile. On the contrary, the institutions of the Republican empire in the provinces were so robust that they were able to withstand the collapse at the centre. Even in the blackest days of civil war there was little question that the provinces would remain loyal to

Rome. Governors governed and rebellions were few. The rule of law was upheld in the provinces; the only major disruption occurred when warring Roman armies rampaged across the landscape. Even then, few provincials and client kings thought of using the breakdown of central government to gain independence from Rome. Instead, they sought to determine which of the warring factions claiming to represent central government should receive their loyalty.

Rome and the army

In a very real sense, Rome was originally run by the army. The main electoral assembly, the *comitia centuriata*, was based on the Roman army, with votes weighted to reflect the military significance of the voters. Cavalrymen had more votes than heavy infantry, whose votes counted for more than the votes of skirmishers.

This made sense when consuls were war leaders, for in an election the army was essentially picking its commander. However, towards the end of the Republic, a fatal disconnection grew between the army and the politicians. The army served further afield, leaving few soldiers in Rome for the elections, meaning that Rome's leaders were not elected by the men who would fight in battle under those leaders. The army was essentially disenfranchised from a process to which its contribution had once been essential. Therefore the soldiers became alienated from the Roman version of democracy and saw little need to support an admittedly corrupt and self-serving system in which they had no say.

Second, the Social War of 90–88 BCE led to the enfranchisement of large numbers of citizens with little experience of democracy but plenty of military experience. These men joined the legions, although they had little loyalty to the city of Rome. Indeed, many had fought Rome just a few years before. They gave their loyalty to their commanders, rather than to the state. Nevertheless, the soldiers who put Sulla, Caesar and Octavian into power were exercising the ancient right of Roman soldiery to choose who would lead Rome and its armies. It may be that the enduring lesson from the fall of the Roman Republic is that if army of a state is not aligned with the democratic process and committed to its preservation, that state will probably not remain a democracy for very long.

2

The early imperial period

Nihil fallacius ratione tota comitiorum. (Nothing is more deceptive than the whole political system).

Cicero, *For Murena* 36

Senators such as the historian Tacitus lamented the loss of liberty that accompanied the fall of the Roman Republic but the governing class of the Republic had not shared much of that liberty. The 'freedom' of the Roman senatorial class was often misused for ruthless exploitation, excessive taxation and arbitrary abuse of power. Politicians in the last century of the Republic habitually reclaimed the heavy financial cost of an electoral campaign from unfortunate taxpayers, and in the provinces these exactions were frequently tyrannical. Even in the early imperial period (approximately 31 BCE–98 CE) financial abuses did not immediately end. Quintilius Varus, the governor of Syria around 6 BCE, is said to have 'entered a rich province as a poor man and left a poor province as a rich man'. Nevertheless, imperial oversight generally kept office-holders in check; over-greedy officials risked massive fines, even their lives.

Although democracy in the city of Rome became a meaningless sham, elsewhere in the empire it remained alive. In Italy, and in the Greek east, candidates still competed in genuinely democratic civic elections. While writers such as the biographer Suetonius concentrated on palace scandal and gossip, contemporary historians paid little attention to the economy of the empire. Archaeological studies have shown that an economic boom quickly raised the population and quality of life in the provinces to a standard not seen again until the early modern era. In short, during the early imperial period people were richer, freer and better-governed, and in many places democracy was stronger. Other than by disaffected senators, 'freedom' was not much missed.

How the provinces were governed

> May it be my privilege to place the State on a firm and stable footing.
>
> Emperor Augustus (Suetonius *Life of Augustus* 28.2)

The smooth transition from Republic to imperial autocracy was due almost entirely to the political skill of Octavian (Augustus). The extent of his skill is shown by how comprehensively his successors bungled the parts of the transition he left unfinished. Following his victory over Mark Antony at Actium, Octavian strove to secure his grip on power. This power was based on the legions, and Octavian wanted those legions securely under his direct command. This meant first putting the army on a financially sound footing and second taking control of the provinces where the legions were to be based. These were his immediate priorities: matters in Rome itself could wait.

Octavian intended to rule most of the empire personally, and certainly those provinces containing substantial military forces. However, the Roman people were innately conservative and strongly distrusted monarchical power. Blatant autocracy had caused the assassination of Julius Caesar and had Octavian boldly proclaimed himself emperor he would not have lasted a week. Therefore he had to find a way to make his rule seem like a return to the constitution and values of the Roman Republic. Octavian achieved this by concealing any constitutional innovations under

Figure 1   For all their apparent realism, statues of Augustus were laden with propaganda. Augustus always appears youthful, and often wears armour or a crown, such as the oak crown given for outstanding civic services. (Picture courtesy of Adrian Goldsworthy)

the guise of the *mos maiorum;* the revered ancestral traditions of Rome.

In Republican times, a man selected to govern a province might not have been able to leave Rome. The *mos maiorum* allowed him to send a *legatus* in his place (from which comes the modern word 'delegate'). Octavian wanted command of about two dozen provinces and their legions but used the Republican convention to send a *Legatus Propraetor Augusti* to actually govern. By delegating governorship, Octavian could reward his allies and simultaneously ease the resentment of the Roman aristocracy at being denied provincial commands. Although *legati* ruled their provinces on behalf of Octavian, the posts remained prestigious,

From Octavian the triumvir to Augustus the emperor

When Caesar made Octavian his heir the young man had to succeed or die. Caesar's deputy, Mark Antony, took power in Rome and refused to allow Octavian access to Caesar's money or documents, forcing the young man to join Antony's enemies. Then in 43 BCE, Octavian abruptly double-crossed his allies, joining forces with Antony and his colleague Lepidus. The three men became 'triumvirs', masters of the Roman world; together, they launched a bloody purge of their enemies.

Octavian took on the difficult task of governing war-torn Italy and coping with Sextus Pompey, son of Pompey the Great, who was based in Sicily, from where he threatened Roman corn supplies. Octavian overcame Pompey with the help of his competent second-in-command, Agrippa, in effect removing Lepidus from the triumvirate. A rebellion in Italy, led by Mark Antony's brother and wife, was also crushed. Finally Octavian turned on Antony himself. Antony had become unpopular due to his alliance and cohabitation with Cleopatra of Egypt. Once Antony had been defeated at Actium in Greece in 31 BCE, Octavian followed him to Egypt. There Antony and Cleopatra committed suicide leaving Octavian free to become Augustus, sole ruler of the Roman world.

financially rewarding and eagerly sought after. Octavian's rule of the provinces was secure but he blunted the charge of autocracy by appearing to share some power. Octavian wanted command of the provinces because of the legions they contained, so he was happy to allow militarily insignificant provinces to be governed by proconsuls as they had been under the Republic. He was thus able to cloak his absolute rule of most of the empire, and particularly his command of its military forces, in quasi-Republican garb. The traditional ways were followed in form if not in substance. In reality, Octavian directly or indirectly exercised personal control of the empire as an imperial autocrat.

Whether they were senatorially appointed proconsuls or imperial propraetors, provincial governors had much the same duties. The Roman Empire was perpetually short of cash so each province had to contribute as much as possible to the imperial exchequer and governors saw to it that the provincials did just that. As injustice created expensive unrest, a governor had to oversee the judicial process. This operated under the *Lex Provinciae*; the code of laws established when the province was constituted, which generally left provincials subject to the laws of the state of which they were citizens. In the early imperial period only a small minority of people in the provinces were Roman citizens.

A governor travelled to at least the major cities in his province once a year, to represent the emperor in legal disputes and at civic functions. Even a peaceful province maintained a small military presence with which the governor could protect villagers and merchants from bandits, and suppress civil disturbances. A governor also commanded the legions in his province. If there were a single legion, he commanded it directly. Otherwise each legion in a province was commanded by a *legatus Augusti legionis*. As this title indicates, though legionary legates were subordinate to the provincial governor, they were appointed by the emperor and answered to him personally. Imperial oversight was made dramatically clear in 47 CE, when Domitius Corbulo, governor of Germania Inferior (Lower Germany) invaded German lands beyond the imperial borders. Sharply ordered back by the emperor Claudius, Corbulo complained furiously (as recorded in Tacitus, *Annals* 11.20) that Republican governors had been lucky men, as they could campaign at will. On his return Corbulo set his legionaries to digging a massive canal between the rivers Meuse and Rhine. The legions were immensely useful for infrastructure development; trained legionaries could be used directly for tasks such as road building or seconded to lend their skills to civic provincial projects. For example, legionary engineers generally oversaw the civilian construction of amphitheatres and aqueducts.

The *civitates* of each province were ruled by town councils, many democratically elected. In areas such as northern Gaul where such *civitates* did not exist, governors actively encouraged their creation. The Roman peace encouraged some peoples to build new cities away from physically secure but uncomfortable hill-forts. In such cities, local aristocrats found new dignity as city officials, which helped their assimilation into the imperial system.

Politics and constitutional developments in Rome

Only the mind of the Divine Augustus could bear such a load.

Emperor Tiberius, on managing the Roman Empire,
Tacitus, *Annals* 1.11

Having never been really broken, provincial governance was easy to fix. Once Octavian had worked out how to govern the provinces of the empire as an autocrat while still appearing to follow Republican convention, the governance of the provinces and civic government in the towns and cities quickly returned to patterns established during the Republic. The problem lay at the centre, where the challenge was essentially to remove the malign effects of a dysfunctional central government that had been poisoning an otherwise workable system. The Roman constitution, so praised two centuries previously by the Greek historian Polybius, had completely broken down. In the later years of the Republic an entrenched and self-interested aristocracy had captured the major offices of state and their cynical abuse of the institutions of democracy had destroyed the credibility of the political process.

To restore central government Octavian faced the same problem as he had in taking control of militarily important provinces. That is, he had to rule as an autocrat while appearing to respect Republican convention. Fortunately there was a solution, and this lay in the same flaws that had allowed the Roman aristocracy to undermine the Republic. Social power in Rome had always trumped political power, so Octavian chose to rule through a combination of patronage, personal extra-constitutional social power and by assuming certain powers without actually holding the political office through which those powers were conventionally wielded. Later as Augustus, Octavian said this explicitly in his *Res Gestae*, the text he left describing his feats to posterity: 'I took precedence over everyone in my personal position (*dignitate*) but I possessed no more [constitutional] power than those who were my colleagues in any magistracy.' This 'personal position' gave the emperor such political and extra-constitutional power that in the later years of his life Octavian/Augustus seldom held the consulship. Instead, he ensured that the highest offices of state were held by men he had selected and who obeyed his bidding.

Nomen Caesaris – **the name of 'Caesar'**

The later historian Cassius Dio imagined one of Octavian's closest advisers, Maecenas, instructing Rome's new emperor on how to cloak his autocratic rule:

> If you think that the title of 'king' is cursed but desire in fact to rule as a monarch, don't call yourself a king but rule under the name of 'Caesar'. If you need more titles your people will call you *imperator* ('emperor') just as they did your father [Octavian's adoptive father, Julius Caesar] ... so you will actually be king in reality without any of the stigma that goes with that name.

Cassius Dio, 52.40

The title of 'imperator' was adopted to become the root of the modern word 'emperor' and Augustus and his successors were called 'the Caesars'. Despite this, because Julius Caesar lacked the powers that Augustus attached to his name, Octavian/Augustus, rather than Julius Caesar, is considered Rome's first emperor.

Octavian did not have a master-plan for remodelling the Roman Empire. Instead by cautious experimentation and improvisation he created what appeared to be a functional republic while actually keeping the apparatus of a military dictatorship intact. In 30 BCE short-term fixes rather than enduring solutions were desperately required. With the army of his defeated rival Mark Antony under his command, Octavian commanded some sixty legions; probably the largest-ever army in Roman history. Demobilisation was a priority, as a near-bankrupt empire could not afford to pay or feed half so many soldiers.

Recent conscripts were sent home, but those without homes had to be found land. Octavian could not afford to have tens of thousands of discontented and desperate men holding a grudge, especially not men skilled in warfare. His solution was pragmatic, brutal and far from painless. The pain was suffered by the municipalities of Italy where large portions of public and private land were taken by forced purchase and handed over to the discharged soldiery. Twenty-eight new colonies of ex-legionaries were founded in Italy, with more abroad from Carthage to Beirut. The wealth of Egypt and the confiscated assets of those who had changed sides too late in the civil wars helped to pay for the expropriated land; so those who were forcibly displaced received some compensation. Nevertheless, the move created considerable hardship and discontent. While this took place, Rome's new master remained outside Italy, 'settling affairs' in the east. In reality, Octavian did little to change the constitutional framework established by Pompey a generation earlier but his absence allowed him to blame subordinates for unpopular decisions. When he returned to Rome, Octavian had himself 'elected' consul, an office he held continuously until 23 BCE. This gave constitutional authority to what had previously been naked autocracy, but continuous consulships were not a long-term solution.

In early January 27 BCE Octavian took the first cautious steps towards creating the appearance of constitutional rule, or as he put it 'restoring the Republic' (*res publica restituta*). However, this phrase implied setting the present Republic on its feet rather than a return to the system of the old Republic. Octavian ostentatiously laid down his dictatorial powers, although at the 'urging' of the senate he allowed himself to become proconsul of those provinces where Rome had a significant military presence. An edict, the *imperium proconsulare*, made official Octavian's power to rule his provinces through praetorian legates. The senate also gave Octavian *maius imperium*: overriding authority over all provincial governors, whether praetorian legates or senatorial proconsuls. As always this innovation was hidden behind Republican precedent, since Pompey had once been given this power. Although the *imperium proconsulare* and *maius imperium* were ostensibly temporary, intended to last for only ten years, their powers were never revoked, and were an essential part of the imperial constitutional framework for centuries. Africa, Macedonia and Illyria were controlled by the senate, despite having legionary garrisons. However the *maius imperium*, together with extra-constitutional pressure on senators in the form of favours, bribes, intimidation and downright coercion, gave the emperor effective control over even the 'senatorial' provinces. In effect Octavian and his successors chose all the provincial governors and intervened in every province of the empire, whether officially in charge or not.

In return for having given up the appearance of autocracy, the senate awarded Octavian a new title: Augustus, the 'revered' or 'illustrious' one. Augustus modestly referred to himself not as king or emperor but as *princeps*, the 'foremost citizen'. From this title comes the name for the form of government he established, the Principate (and also the later title of 'prince'). The deliberate ambiguity of Augustus' constitutional role was tested early. Marcus Primus, the senatorial governor of Macedonia, invaded Thrace. The senate, not Augustus, oversaw Primus. If Primus had acted without orders from Augustus, the emperor's unofficial position as commander-in-chief of the army would have been undermined. If Augustus had told Primus to invade Thrace, he would have exceeded his authority. In the end, the senate (undoubtedly at Augustus' private urging) charged Primus with exceeding his authority. Augustus testified that he had not influenced Primus one way or the other and Primus was condemned to death.

Augustus jealously guarded his relationship with the legions. When a later governor of Macedonia crushed an enemy army and personally killed its leader he was entitled to the *spolia optima*, an honour awarded only twice in Roman history. However, the glorification of a general who was not Augustus was completely unacceptable. A pretext was found to deny granting the *spolia optima* and the governor was given an ordinary triumph; one of the last to be celebrated by a Roman who was not of the imperial family. Thereafter victorious generals were allowed only triumphal ornaments, the signs of distinction they would afterwards have possessed had they actually celebrated their triumph.

Augustus left Rome for the provinces in 27 BCE. The military situation in Hispania and Gaul needed attention and Augustus preferred to lead the army personally whenever possible. He may also have been consciously emulating the great Greek lawgiver Solon, who, having settled constitutional matters in Athens, left the city in order to make it harder for those changes to be undone. While Augustus was away from Rome elections and meetings of the senate followed the old constitutional pattern. The old Republic was dead, but the absence of the emperor allowed a credible semblance to thrive. In 23 BCE Augustus suffered an illness so severe that he nearly died. Agrippa was given Augustus' ring and briefed, as far as Augustus could manage, on the current state of the empire but it was doubtful whether the army and senate would accept Agrippa as Augustus' successor.

Fortunately, Augustus made a full recovery. Nevertheless he decided to make further changes. Up to this point Augustus had held one consulship and rewarded a close ally with the other;

this denied the top offices of state to men whose families had occupied them for generations. Augustus' absence from Rome had allowed certain conspirators to exploit this senatorial resentment. Augustus was too shrewd a ruler not to have an effective intelligence service and the plotters were quickly discovered and executed, but Augustus now addressed the root of the problem and resigned the consulship. Although his powers of *maius imperium* and *imperium proconsulare* in the provinces were undiminished by this resignation, the old Republic had denied provincial governors any powers in the city of Rome itself, for exactly the reasons that Augustus now wanted them.

By resigning from the consulship, the proconsular authority of Augustus lapsed while he was within Rome. Therefore before resigning he arranged for the senate to make an exception and allow his authority to remain in force. By resigning as consul Augustus also gave up his authority over the senate, so he 'temporarily' took the *tribunicia potestas*, the powers of a tribune. This was a shrewd move, for the tribunes traditionally protected the common man and the common man trusted Augustus far more than the senate. Also someone with authority enough to use the constitutional powers of the tribunate to the full – as the Gracchus brothers had proven a century before – could so dominate the senate that enemies called them 'kings of Rome'. Tribunican power allowed Augustus to summon the senate, veto laws and even arrest the consuls should he so desire. This power combined with his extra-constitutional powers of patronage and coercion to make the emperor supreme in Rome. Enhanced provincial powers gave Augustus control of over twenty legions. This, combined with his authority in Rome, made his position unassailable.

Yet the emperor's true power lay outside the constitution. Augustus had sufficient powers of patronage and punishment to suborn or terrorise the staunchest republican. Where necessary his immense wealth could buy support and trade it for political offices and provincial commands. The emperor's backing made

The Varian disaster

'Quintilius Varus, give me back my legions!' Thus, Suetonius, in his *Life of Augustus* 23.2, reports Augustus' reaction to hearing that three Romans legions had been wiped out.

Germany was close to becoming a Roman province by 9 CE, until expansion was halted by a massive rebellion in the Balkans. This rebellion drew away more than half of the legions, leaving Germany with just the governor Quintilius Varus and three legions. Varus was no military man and he placed his trust – wrongly – in Arminius, a German aristocrat who had grown up in Rome and returned to Germania as a Roman officer.

Arminius established a seditious confederation of tribes to expel Rome from his homeland. False reports of a minor rebellion deceived Varus into moving his army through the Teutoburg forest. At Kalkriese, the Germans ambushed the unsuspecting Romans who were caught between a bog and the forest. Roman efforts to fight off the ambushers were hampered by heavy rain and German defences which prevented them from breaking out of the trap.

Three complete legions – the seventeenth, eighteenth and nineteenth – were wiped out and Varus committed suicide. This was the largest Roman defeat since Hannibal's victory at Cannae; Rome never regained its conquests beyond the Rhine.

a senator's career, just as imperial enmity would break it. Everyone knew that behind the benevolent *pater patriae* 'the father of his country' stretched the shadow of Octavian, the bloodstained triumvir. Rome's ruler had been calculating and pitiless while striving for power and would undoubtedly be equally merciless if his power were challenged. There were few challengers.

Augustus had squared the constitutional circle to his own satisfaction, yet he left huge problems for his successors, including the problem of how that successor was to be designated. His determination not to be seen as an autocrat caused Augustus to make the position of emperor an informal, extra-constitutional office. He could hardly designate a successor to an office that did not exist. The question of who could become an emperor was left

Lex de Imperio Vespasiani – **imperial powers as law**

In 69 CE Vespasian appears to have received his powers en bloc, either by law or through a decree of the senate. Much of the inscription containing the essential details has been lost, and the surviving portion does not make clear whether proconsular imperium and tribunican powers were awarded at this point. It is also unclear whether the award was made to Vespasian personally or acknowledged that all future emperors required these powers to do their job. Nevertheless, this 'law' officially recognised that such a person as an emperor existed and needed to govern. This was a large step away from the informal principate of Augustus and towards the recognition of emperor as a constitutional office.

open and while it was frequently debated (often at sword-point, by entire armies) it was never satisfactorily resolved. Also, because the *princeps* was invisible to the formal constitution, his relationship with the senate was undefined. Rome needed senators to command armies, run provinces and propose legislation, not least because both senators and citizens expected that senators would do this. To what extent the emperor could instruct the senate what to do, and how respectfully he should give those instructions, were matters every emperor and senate had to resolve. Three times during the principate, that resolution was achieved by the emperor's death – Caius Caligula, Nero and Domitian – although many senators also perished along the way.

Family matters

> I wish I had been her father
>
> > Augustus' comment on a woman who hanged herself
> > Suetonius, *Life of Augustus* 65.2

While Romans were deeply suspicious of kings, they were oddly comfortable with a royal family. In every generation in

Republican Rome the top jobs in Rome were held by a Servil-
ius, a Scipio, a Metellus or another of the favoured few whom
Cicero had described as made 'consuls in their cradles'. Dynasties
were not a novelty and therefore acceptable to the conservative
Roman mind.

As Caesar's adopted son, Augustus (Octavian) had joined
that favoured elite. Octavian's then wife offered him no political
benefits in these circles, so he divorced her on the very day she
gave birth to his daughter, Julia. In 39 BCE he took the next step
through his marriage to the Claudian aristocrat Livia Drusilla,
so joining the Julian family with one even more distinguished.
This although Livia was already married; indeed pregnant. Not
unexpectedly her current husband agreed to a quick divorce and
a few days after her son was born Livia wed Augustus. To Julia, the
daughter he had already, Augustus was a strict father:

> He made his daughter and his granddaughters learn
> spinning and weaving as part of their upbringing. They
> were forbidden to say or do anything that could not be
> recorded in the household diary. They were totally barred
> from meeting strangers.
>
> Suetonius, *Life of Augustus* 64.2

Augustus and Livia had no children, but none the less their
marriage endured for half a century. In his later years Augustus
knew that he needed an heir if his principate was to endure.
Consequently, in 23 BCE, he married Julia to a close relative and
the most eligible bachelor in Rome, Claudius Marcellus. Both
newly-weds were young: Julia was fourteen and her husband
about seventeen but in ancient Rome death claimed the young
as often as the old; Julia was widowed at sixteen. Augustus' faithful
henchman Agrippa became the emperor's next son-in-law and
heir (and his presumed successor as emperor). The marriage was
productive – five children were born to them – but not happy.

Julia resented having a husband twenty-five years her senior and also rebelled against her restrictive upbringing in a string of affairs, which Agrippa diplomatically overlooked:

> Despite her notorious infidelities, all Julia's children closely resembled Agrippa. At a dinner party, a close friend asked how this could be so and received the crisp answer 'A wise captain does not allow passengers on board until the cargo is in the hold.'
>
> Macrobius, *Saturnalia*, I2, 5

As his health was always poor, Augustus did not account for the one factor that continually frustrated his plans for the succession: his longevity. When Agrippa died in 12 BCE Augustus looked to his stepson Tiberius as a possible successor. Despite his outstanding lack of charisma, Tiberius was a solid general and his personal integrity was undoubted. Both he and his brother Drusus – an outstandingly successful general – were in line for the imperial succession but in 9 BCE Drusus was thrown from his horse and died from complications of a compound fracture of the thigh.

Augustus, perhaps inspired by the successful marriage of Livia's younger son Drusus to Mark Antony's daughter, his niece Antonia, ordered Julia to wed Tiberius. To marry his stepsister Tiberius had to divorce his wife, Agrippa's daughter Vipsania, whom he loved. As a proud Claudian who anyway resented his new bride, Tiberius was not disposed to overlook his wife's infidelity and the couple's marriage was stormy. Perhaps because of Julia's complaints Augustus cooled towards the idea of Tiberius as a successor, instead favouring his grandchildren, Gaius and Lucius, the sons of Julia and Agrippa. Partly because of this and partly because he could not stand his wife, Tiberius resigned his public offices and took himself to self-imposed exile on the island of Rhodes where he remained for almost a decade.

Two things brought Tiberius back to Rome. First, Julia's misconduct had become flagrant: 'She left untried no obscenity

Figure 2 Marcus Vipsanius Agrippa was the executive power behind the success of the new regime. A highly competent general and administrator, his death left a gaping hole in Augustus' dynastic plans. (Picture courtesy of Adrian Goldsworthy)

of which a woman could be guilty either as perpetrator or object; setting up her own caprice as a law unto herself', remarked the historian Velleius Paterculus (*Roman History* 2.100). Later writers expanded this to allege that Julia prostituted herself under a statue of the satyr Marsayas in the forum and enjoyed nightly debaucheries. Eventually a scandalised Augustus exiled his wayward daughter to an island off the Italian coast.

The second reason for recalling Tiberius was that both Augustus' grandchildren, Gaius and Lucius, had died young. This was not unusual given the mortality rate in Rome. As part of his imperial training Gaius had been in nominal command of a minor war in the far east, where, in 4 CE, he succumbed to a javelin wound. Lucius – probably – perished from disease: 'His death was due to a sudden illness. In connection with both deaths therefore, suspicion attached to Livia both at the time and in later ages', the historian Cassius Dio (55.10) darkly remarked. Livia's malign hand was alleged to lie behind these deaths, which some believed to be poisonings intended to ensure that her son Tiberius became emperor. This is unlikely but the truth will never be known for poisoning is hard to prove in an era when, for example, a burst appendix could be fatal.

Fate, or Livia, had determined that Augustus had only one choice of heir. Tiberius would succeed Augustus and in turn be succeeded by Germanicus, the flamboyant and popular son of Tiberius' dead brother Drusus. Augustus adopted Tiberius as his son, officially making him a member of the Julian family. In 7 CE, Tiberius received the same tribunican powers as Augustus and in 13 CE, the *maius imperium* which gave him precedence over provincial governors and made him officially Augustus' equal. However the social pressure that subordinated a son to his father meant that in reality Augustus remained unambiguously in charge. Nevertheless, Augustus had arranged matters so that when he died in 14 CE, Tiberius needed no further powers or endorsement. He had been pre-crowned.

The Julio-Claudian dynasty

> The provinces were not unhappy with the new condition of affairs. They had distrusted government by the Senate and [Roman] people, because rivalry among the aristocracy and the rapacity of officialdom had made the protection of the laws insufficient.
>
> Tacitus, *Annals* 1.2

Tiberius' rule began with the assassination of the last surviving grandson of Augustus, Agrippa Postumus. Any male member of the imperial family was qualified to be emperor, so relatives were now rivals. This flaw in the imperial system sucked the Julio-Claudian dynasty into a spiral of internecine assassinations and executions, as suspicion led to pre-emptive strikes and a complete breakdown of family trust. The entire imperial clan wiped itself out within three generations. The colourful lives of the later Julio-Claudians (that is, the successors of Tiberius) are legend. Popular belief has Caligula the mad emperor followed by dithering Claudius (and his nymphomaniac teenage wife Messalina) and finally by the matricidal orgy-loving Nero, who burned Christians and most of Rome. In 68 CE the last surviving male Julio-Claudian took the process to its logical extreme by committing suicide.

The combined reigns of Augustus and Tiberius lasted sixty-one years, while Caius Caligula, Claudius and Nero together reigned from 37 to 68 CE; half as long. For its first two generations, the empire was governed by steady emperors who encouraged population and economic growth. So prosperous did the empire become that, writing just after the end of the Julio-Claudian era, the biographer Suetonius remarked of the imperial household of Augustus: 'The simplicity of his furniture and household goods may be seen from couches and tables still in existence, many of which are scarcely fine enough for a private citizen today' (*Life of Augustus* 73).

Other than Nero, who although much maligned was genuinely awful, the legends of imperial debauchery mostly have a flimsy basis. Most of the excesses of Caius Caligula are either unproven or fictions by senatorial writers (the senate loathed him). The history of this period was written by senators and they used the rich and often scatological Roman tradition of political abuse to attack the reputation of Caius Caligula and his family with any mud they thought would stick. (In the Republican era, Cicero cheerfully used demonstrably untrue allegations to denounce his enemies as parricides, gladiators and arsonists.) Accounts of the more bizarre misdeeds of the Julio-Claudians must be read with caution: Suetonius and his ilk had no compunction about libel. Caligula did not make his horse a consul; even his enemies admitted he was not interested in orgies;

he was a loving father and his known victims number twenty-six. (Both Caligula's predecessor Tiberius and his successor Claudius slaughtered well into treble figures.) This 'restraint' is partly because Caius Caligula's reign was short, from 37 to 41 CE. It is significant that though the senate rejoiced at the killing of the tyrannical madman who had usurped their power, the common people of Rome were displeased.

Likewise the – probably genuine – personal foibles of Emperor Claudius had little effect on the empire. While historians ancient and modern debate whether Messalina's sexual depravity was genuine, fewer emphasise the genuine achievements of Claudius' reign. The seaport of Ostia is a notable example. This was substantially rebuilt, moving the main harbour from the river mouth to a natural bay just over a mile away. The size of the bay was greatly increased by breakwaters created using the recent innovation of concrete that could set under water. The development of Ostia was mirrored by infrastructure developments across the Mediterranean, creating trade and social links that bound the provinces in an ever-closer union. In contrast to these important developments the antics of the Julio-Claudian court mattered little, as some recognised even at the time. According to the historian Tacitus, the Roman general Petellius Cerialis told rebellious Gauls:

> From worthy Emperors you derive the same advantages [as those living in Rome], though you dwell so far away. However cruel rulers are most dangerous to those who have to live close to them. Endure the whims and rapacity of such masters, just as you put up with seasons of droughts and excessive rain and other natural disasters, for there will be vices as long as there are men. But such men don't last forever and even the worst rule offers good things in compensation.

Tacitus, *Histories* 74ff.

Those 'good things' included the protection of the legions against invading Germans and the suppression of the inter-tribal wars that had plagued Gaul since time immemorial. The taxes that supported the legions and paid for the amenities of Roman civilization – roads, international trade and an equitable and transparent legal system – were covered by the savings from the wars the Gauls no longer had to fight. Modern historians have largely had to unearth Gaul's increasing prosperity throughout the first and second centuries from the archaeological record; Roman historians and biographers were more preoccupied with palace scandals, such as possible poisonings by Livia and the number of Messalina's lovers.

Despite accounts of senators perishing by the dozen as collateral damage in Julio-Claudian court intrigues, not until Nero do we hear of substantial misgovernment of the empire as a whole. Most provinces were governed better than they had been in the Republic, not least because governors knew that summary – sometimes very summary – justice awaited them in Rome. The senatorial historical tradition is scathingly bitter about wives and freedmen pre-empting the senate's job. If Claudius was indeed a weak ruler, and many decisions were actually made by his freedman Pallas or by Agrippina Minor (who Claudius married after Messalina's execution), it is significant that the sources criticise those who took the decisions, rather than asserting that the decisions themselves were bad, which generally they were not.

Economic development

Pecunia non olet. (Money does not stink)

Proverb attributed to the emperor Vespasian (69–79 CE),
who instituted a tax on urinals

Imperial fiscal policy was basically household management on a large scale, which is exactly what *oiko nomia* 'the regulation of the house' means. This had been good enough for the Republic and Augustus made few changes. Paying for the army was always the Roman Empire's greatest expense, so in 6 CE Augustus established the *aerarium militare*, the military treasury of Rome. This was paid for by a tax on inheritance and a sales duty but also largely by donations from the emperor's personal wealth, which greatly strengthened the personal bond between emperor and army. The fund not only paid soldiers their salary but also provided a pension fund for disabled soldiers. This change was an implicit admission that Rome's armies would no longer be funded by the booty of conquest and that in many areas the Roman Empire's borders had reached their natural limits.

If pay for the army was the first priority, infrastructure development came second. Under Augustus and his immediate successors, roads, bridges and harbours were repaired and developed and civic leaders were encouraged to undertake their own building projects. New amphitheatres and basilicas arose and temples were either constructed or extensively renovated. Augustus famously boasted that he 'found Rome a city of brick and left it a city of marble'. Augustus' henchman Agrippa built the Pantheon which – after being extensively renovated by Hadrian – stands almost totally intact in Rome today. Augustus also claimed to have restored another eighty-two temples. The Aqua Julia, Anio Vetus, Marcia and Appia aqueducts were renovated or rebuilt and Augustus built an entire new forum in central Rome between the old forum and the Esquiline hill. These achievements were mirrored in towns and cities across the empire.

Building projects were enormously expensive (it was proverbial among the Roman aristocracy that a passion for building led to financial ruin). However, construction created what modern economists would call 'velocity in the money supply'. Building projects created jobs and those with those jobs spent money on other things. This led to increased prosperity, an increase in tax revenues and money available for further building projects.

Prosperity increased demand for manufactured goods just as improved roads and harbours enabled the easy transport of these goods. At the same time greater wealth lowered civil unrest and the cost of policing the populace, releasing funds for more productive uses. In short, the imperial peace released a pent-up need for goods, services and infrastructure development. Augustus provided the initial fiscal stimulus from tribute and booty from his campaigns, especially his capture of Egypt. Thereafter the empire settled into a virtuous circle in which economic development itself spurred further progress.

Agriculture

> So in old age, you happy man, your fields will still be yours and ample for your need!
>
> Virgil, *Eclogue* 1.46

As in every era before the modern, most people were farmers. Historians disagree about whether farmers generally lived within their township and commuted to their fields, or lived on the land they farmed. No doubt those within convenient distance of city walls preferred to live within them and in militarily insecure border areas some dwelt in the city even if it was inconvenient. However villa farmhouses unearthed by archaeologists show that some farmers lived permanently outside the city. Among urban poets and aristocrats, this rustic existence was the ideal:

> This was my prayer: a patch of land, modestly sized,
> With a garden and a spring always running near the house,
> And above that a small wood.
>
> Horace, *Satires* 2.6.1–3

In reality, the vagaries of the weather, crop diseases and parasite infestations made country life far from idyllic. Country life was hard enough to force many into the cities or the army. Many who remained on the land were slaves with little choice in the matter. This was particularly true of *latifundia*, huge estates that wealthy absentee landlords farmed with slave labour, with some slaves treated worse than the cattle they herded. *Latifundia* were a common and growing phenomenon. However, the decline of the peasant farmer was not as precipitous as once assumed. Despite the elder Pliny's observation that '*latifundia* are the ruin of Italy' archaeology shows that some smallholdings continued to thrive and indeed constituted the majority of agricultural producers.

A soldier, Columella, took up farming in the time of Nero. He produced a book, *On Farming*, and a smaller treatise on the management of woodlands. These books give us a unique insight into Roman agricultural practices:

> One bull is quite enough for fifteen cows and the sex of the offspring to be born is clear. If the bull dismounts on the right side, he has begotten a male and on the left a female ... Where fodder is abundant, a calf can be bred from the mother every year, otherwise every second year at most. Also a cow can be put to work or used to yield milk but not both.

> Columella, *On Farming* 6.26.5

Alongside peasant smallholdings, and partly replacing them in some areas, specialist crops were grown for the new markets created by the ease of international trade. The coastal areas of North Africa and the flood plains of Egypt were better suited to large-scale grain production than much of Italy, so while imported grain replaced Italian crops many Italians turned to large-scale viticulture. The emperor Domitian (81–96 CE) ordered some vineyards destroyed, possibly because he feared that Italy was too dependent on grain imports. He may also have remembered that as a rebel general his father Vespasian had cut off Italy's corn

Advice for Roman bee-keepers

Bees which come to us by gift or by capture should be accepted with less scrutiny, although even in these circumstances I would not care to possess any but the best, since good and bad bees cost their keeper the same amount of money and labour; also (and this is especially important) inferior bees should not be mixed with those of high quality, since they bring down the overall standard. A smaller yield of honey rewards your efforts when the idler swarms take part in the gathering of it. Nevertheless since sometimes, owing to local conditions, an indifferent set of bees has to be procured (though never on any account should you acquire a bad one), we should take care in seeking out swarms by the following method. Wherever there are suitable woodlands where honey can be gathered, there is nothing that the bees would sooner do than choose springs near at hand for their use.

Columella, *On Farming* 9.8.5–8

supply. North Africa also became a major supplier of olives to the Italian market, creating a number of millionaires in the process.

One might expect that Gaul, and later Britain, would be highly productive agriculturally, as these lands are today. However, the Romans had not invented the horse-collar and without it the heavy northern clays could not easily be ploughed. Furthermore the export of agricultural produce by sea was financially not viable for Britain and Gaul, and far from risk-free elsewhere. Though subdued from the excesses of the first century BCE, piracy remained an issue; the elder Pliny's command of the fleet at Misenum was partly to suppress pirates. Though sea traffic was vastly swifter and cheaper than land haulage, it was only possible between March and November and even then the direction of trade depended on ocean currents and prevailing winds. To encourage Rome's proto-capitalists to invest in the Egyptian grain trade, the emperors guaranteed the price of grain on arrival in Italy and provided rudimentary insurance for ships which failed to complete the journey.

Manufacturing

Our iron age praises not love but loot.

Tibullus, *Elegies* 2.3.40

International trade developed almost as soon as sailing was invented. Long before the foundation of Rome, Egyptian Pharaohs were buried with chariots made from elm, willow and other imported woods unobtainable in Egypt. In later centuries under the *Pax Romana* (the Roman peace) trade across the Mediterranean basin developed substantially, both in agricultural produce and manufactured goods.

Two items, oil lamps and earthenware, are readily tracked, as they were made of baked clay, which is essentially indestructible (they can be broken but the shards do not decompose). Oil lamps made to a standard design were usually marked with a manufacturer's symbol. Products from these 'factories' have been found across the empire and beyond, giving modern archaeologists an insight into trade patterns in antiquity. Earthenware crockery shared the durability and ubiquity of oil lamps. Distinctive 'red-figure' ware from factories in Arretium and Puetoli has been unearthed from Britain to Mesopotamia.

The role of 'factories' should not be over emphasised. Production by individual artisans remained the norm, as demonstrated in Herculaneum and Pompeii where time essentially stopped in 79 CE when both cities were buried to a depth of six metres by the eruption of Vesuvius (which also claimed the life of the elder Pliny). It is almost certain that every city in the empire had the same small workshops as these two cities, where individual craftsmen produced and sold items from shops opening on to the street. Many craftsmen were slaves who operated semi-independently and were paid a small wage (*peculium*) by their masters. Slavery kept the cost of goods and services low and left little incentive for labour-saving innovations. Suetonius tells of 'a mechanical engineer, who promised to transport some heavy columns to the Capitol at small expense'. Vespasian rewarded the man substantially but refused to use the invention, saying: 'You must let me feed my poor working people' (Suetonius, *Life of Vespasian* 18).

Regional specialisation developed during the early imperial period. Egypt had a monopoly on papyrus and Hispania produced massive amounts of *garum*, a highly-spiced fish sauce. Amphorae which had contained imports of this fish sauce or of olive oil were dumped between the Aventine hill and the Tiber docks. Today, they form a small hill (and priceless archaeological resource) known as Monte Testaccio. Exotic products, from spices to silk underwear came from further east. Ports such as Ephesus received regular caravans from Parthia bringing goods from further down the Silk Road which stretched through central Asia to China and beyond: the pepper used to spice Roman meals came from or around the island of Java.

The tumultuous sixties

> When three times three centuries have run their course, Rome will perish through civil strife.
>
>> Prophecy circulating in the reign of Nero (nine hundred years after the traditional date of the founding of Rome)
>
>> Cassius Dio, 62.18

In the final decades of the Julio-Claudian dynasty, selecting an emperor was reduced to choosing whichever family member was still standing. By 54 CE this meant Domitius Nero, a direct descendant of Augustus on the maternal line and adopted son of the emperor Claudius. Political intrigue, poisoning and summary execution had made the once-prolific Julio-Claudians increasingly scarce. Nero and his stepbrother Britannicus were the only available choices and Britannicus was not yet an adult. The imperial office had no apparatus for an orderly, constitutional handover of power, so once chosen, emperors tended to briskly eliminate alternative candidates, which naturally included family members. Nero eventually completed the extinction of the Julio-Claudian line by killing (among many others) his mother, his stepbrother, his wife and ultimately himself.

In contrast to this chaotic and dysfunctional system at the top, by and large competent appointees commanded the legions and provinces. Nero changed this, being both incompetent at governance and murderously disinclined to let anyone more capable do the job. He forced his chief advisor Seneca to commit suicide, while Corbulo, a highly competent general, was executed mainly because of his popularity with the army. Where previous imperial shenanigans had affected only the capital, Nero's malign influence affected the entire empire. There was relatively little unrest

Boudicca

Suetonius Paulinus was Nero's governor in Britain, a province added to the empire under Claudius in 43 CE. Paulinus ignored illegal land seizures by retired legionaries in eastern Britain and the growing resentment of local elites. At the sensitive moment when the pro-Roman Prasutagus, king of the Iceni, died, Paulinus stripped eastern Britain of troops for a campaign on the other side of the island.

Roman officials came to collect the emperor's share of Prasutagus' will. Thanks to the blind and brutal arrogance of the imperial procurator (the man who represented the emperor's financial interests in a province), Prasutagus' estate was pillaged, his widow whipped and his two daughters raped.

His widow, Boudicca, capitalising on resentment of Rome, raised a massive army. This army destroyed much of the local Ninth legion and flattened Colchester, Londinium and Verulamium (St Albans). Boudicca was eventually brought to battle and her army destroyed, but by then depopulation and economic devastation had set back the development of Britannia by a generation.

in the provinces before Nero's time but his bad governors and worse policies quickly changed that.

The senators resented the loss of their traditional power, making their relations with the Julio-Claudian emperors generally fraught. Caius Caligula feuded with the senate, the major reason why contemporary historians – who were senators – gave him such a bad press. Under Nero, relationships with the senate reached new lows. In part this was because Nero's family, other than Nero himself, was basically extinct. After Nero the next emperor would be a senator, since at this time neither the army nor the general population would contemplate being ruled by anyone else. By killing family members to remove threats to their own position, the Julio-Claudians had transferred the threat from their immediate family to an entire social class. Undaunted, Nero set about destroying the credibility of the senatorial institution, since by harming the entire senatorial class he was harming his successor and rival, whoever that might be. Senators and their families were forced to participate in orgies and to fight in the arena as gladiators.

Egoism, as much as dynastic insecurity, helped Nero's downfall. In 64 CE Rome was devastated by a huge fire. With much of the city destroyed, Nero decided to rebuild it in a manner befitting his imperial capital. Though this rebuilding had many positive aspects, they were more than counterbalanced by the splendid palace, the *Domus Aurea* (the Golden House), that Nero built for himself. So large and extravagant was this palace that Romans suspected the fire had been deliberately started to make room for it. Meanwhile, the provincials resented the increased taxes which paid for reconstruction work. By 67 CE Nero was hated by the Roman plebs, by provincials and by the senate. This might not have mattered, but this most unmilitary of emperors was also despised by the army for his debauched lifestyle.

After Boudicca's uprising in Britain, another rebellion developed. Judea was a combination of province and client kingdom.

Order was kept by Roman soldiers and an imperial official was responsible for these men and for tax collection. (One such official was Pontius Pilate, who had supervised the execution in 32 CE of a man called Jesus, who he considered to be a Jewish troublemaker.) Roman rule, however indirect, aggrieved a people who had resisted invaders for a thousand years. Rebels and bandits in the countryside made farming dangerous and unprofitable. Imperial taxes were raised to offset the lost income from failed farms, forcing more farmers into bankruptcy or banditry. Rebellion finally broke out in 66 CE when tensions between Greeks and Jews in the coastal city of Caesarea erupted into riots which rapidly developed into a general uprising. The ad hoc nature of the rebellion led to widespread internecine fighting among Jewish factions with differing agendas.

To restore the peace, Cestius Gallus, the governor of Syria, advanced into Judea with the Twelfth legion. However he was as unprepared as the rebels had been and although he briefly besieged Jerusalem, a lack of supplies forced him to withdraw. At the pass of Beth Huron his legion was ambushed and almost wiped out. Thereafter, to crush the revolt, Nero sent an army under the command of Vespasian, a general who had distinguished himself during the conquest of Britain. Nero cherished the (futile) hope that Vespasian could be entrusted with an army because his undistinguished ancestry disqualified him as a potential emperor. In 67 CE Vespasian began by methodically crushing resistance in Galilee. The historian Josephus has left an eyewitness account of the fighting, including a description of the Roman siege of Jotapa, which is unique in being the only account of an attack by the Roman army from the receiving end. It includes the chilling account of a man decapitated by a catapult stone. Preserved by his helmet, the man's head was later found intact several hundred feet away.

Any satisfaction Nero might have felt at Vespasian's progress was soon overshadowed by bad news from elsewhere. In 68 CE a Gallic nobleman called Vindex rose in revolt against Nero.

The rebellion was minor and easily crushed but the ambiguous response of the legions underscored Nero's unpopularity with the army. Unlike his predecessors, Nero had never participated in a campaign or even made a serious inspection of field legions. Instead he had acted on the stage at a time when actors made up a despised rank of society. This upset the mostly straitlaced population of rural recruits and provincials who already took a dim view of Nero's well-advertised homosexual affairs and general debaucheries. Consequently when Sulpicius Galba declared his intention to rule his province of Spain 'for the senate and people of Rome', Nero was unable to counter this direct challenge. The army immediately went over the rebel side and the senate declared Nero an outlaw. Abandoned even by his servants, Nero fled Rome (where the common people rioted against him and pulled down his statues) and committed suicide in a villa just outside the city. His last words were famously 'What an artist dies with me!'; an awed comment on the plans that he had quickly made for his tomb.

Nero, self-proclaimed 'creative genius'

Nero fancied himself as a follower of the muses. He not only wrote epic poetry but shocked and embarrassed the empire by performing it on stage, accompanying himself on the harp. Senators were compelled to attend these events. According to contemporary accounts Nero had a weak voice and his poetry was so dire that a member of the audience allegedly faked his own death to get out of the theatre. Nevertheless, Nero was so deluded about his ability that towards the end of his reign he talked of retiring to become a musician in Alexandria.

Coins from Nero's reign are among the most handsome ever produced and probably do reflect the emperor's personal taste, for Nero had some flair for the visual arts. However, these beautiful coins were made with debased metal, for Nero was illiterate in matters economic and financial.

After Nero came the memorable year 69 CE: the 'year of the four emperors'. Galba had the experience to make a good ruler and his Sulpician family was one of the noblest in Rome. 'He would have been thought a great emperor had he never ruled', remarked Tacitus, who as a child personally experienced Galba's rule, which lasted for all of six months. Galba was a rigid aristocrat who never grasped the importance of pleasing the army that had brought him to power. 'I choose my soldiers – I do not buy them', he declared haughtily.

Galba soon faced two military rebellions, one by the army in Germany and a coup by the Praetorian Guard in Rome. The Praetorian coup in which Galba was killed, was led by Otho, a supporter understandably miffed because the seventy-year-old Galba did not make him his successor. Understandably, because Otho was the popular choice and the logic of empire dictated that Galba's nominee would execute Otho as soon as Galba died, Otho opted for a pre-emptive strike; Galba was killed by the praetorians. Otho took command in Rome and immediately led his praetorians against the rebel German legions. These, led by provincial governor Lucius Vitellius, met near the city of Cremona on 14 April, 69 CE. Neither Otho nor Vitellius was present at the battle but Otho was appalled both by the defeat of his army and because Romans were slaughtering each other. He committed suicide, handing Vitellius the empire by default.

Meanwhile Vespasian had reduced the Jewish rebellion to the siege of Jerusalem. His legions represented one of the largest concentrations of military force in the empire, so many defeated Othonians transferred their loyalty to Vespasian. Whether he wanted to become emperor or not, Vespasian became a serious candidate and therefore had to become Caesar or die. Most of the subsequent fighting on Vespasian's side was done by Antonius Primus, an impetuous legionary legate who seized command of legions from Pannonia and marched on Italy. Primus broke the German legions in a second battle not far from the first at

Cremona and went on to take Rome. Vitellius was captured and lynched by Primus' men, allowing Vespasian and his family to take control of the empire.

The Flavian dynasty

> The Flavian family ... restored the empire to peace and security. Their lineage was indeed obscure and without ancestral honours; but the public had no cause to regret its elevation.
>
> Suetonius, *Life of Vespasian* 1.1

The civil wars of 69 CE again exposed the great flaw of the principate. An emperor had either to dispose of potential rivals or risk being overthrown by them. Over the centuries this killed many emperors, their relatives and popular military commanders. This period also revealed what Tacitus called 'a secret of empire': that emperors could be made outside Rome, by the army. This time also marks the point where the city of Rome began, almost imperceptibly, to cease to be the focus of power in the empire; a process which continued over the centuries until Rome, although a great city, was not even one of the imperial capitals.

After 69 CE the empire was no longer the family possession of the Julio-Claudians. This led to the further evolution of the office of *princeps*. Even as Galba began his march on Rome, he unilaterally adopted himself into the Julian family, calling himself 'Caesar' and making this a rank rather than a family name. By making himself heir to the Julian name Galba inherited the immense personal wealth of the Julio-Claudian emperors. There had been no distinction between imperial and Julio-Claudian family assets, because Nero, the last scion of the Julian house, had owned the lot. After 69 CE this imperial patrimony traditionally went to the next emperor, however he came by the title.

Vespasian did not immediately collect all the titles and powers that went with his office but caused the senate to vote them to him over the following months. He immediately acquired the *maius imperium* and proconsular powers, as these were essential for control of the empire. However as Vespasian was outside Rome for the first months of his rule he had no use for the tribunican powers which could only be used within Rome itself. The senate gave him this power when he arrived in Rome. This became standard practice; the emperor became emperor as soon as he had been acknowledged by the army and senate. Then, depending on which of the two bodies he most needed to flatter, he dated the start of his reign from that acknowledgement. His constitutional powers would be awarded later, as and when necessary.

Flavius Vespasian is unambiguously of the small group that history recognises as 'good emperors', although his cheerful, earthy demeanour masked a subtle and ruthless politician. Vespasian sought reconciliation with the senate and endeared himself to the Roman plebs by partly demolishing Nero's Golden House and opening the rest to the public. He drained the ornamental lake outside the grandiose mansion and replaced it with the massive amphitheatre that now symbolises the city of Rome, the *amphitheatrum Flavium*, or Colosseum. Later, Vespasian's son Domitian added to the monumental architecture of the city, creating an arch between the Colosseum and forum to commemorate his brother and father's triumph over the rebellious Jews and the sack of Jerusalem.

In getting the empire's straitened finances in order, Vespasian became famous for his tight-fistedness. He taxed the use of public urinals (which bore the name of *vespasienne* in France until the twenty-first century). Profiteering provincial governors were recalled to Rome and stripped of their wealth with massive fines. These governors were called Vespasian's 'sponges' because they soaked up wealth in the provinces before being squeezed dry in Rome. A side effect of the dysfunctional imperial succession was that an emperor had to make his son his heir, since no other emperor would allow so well-qualified a rival to live. Vespasian's son Titus duly inherited the empire and was fondly remembered; possibly because his reign was brief; from 79 to 81 CE. Had Nero or Caius Caligula ruled for only two years they too would have died well-regarded.

Titus underwent a post mortem examination, probably to exonerate Domitian of blame for his brother's death. (The post mortem uncovered a growth in Titus' brain, which strongly suggests that he died of cancer.) Nevertheless, to ensure that no one pre-empted his succession, Domitian spent the hours before his brother's death not at his bedside, but at the barracks of the Praetorian guard. Domitian reigned for fifteen years, longer than any emperor since Tiberius. So unlike the short-lived Titus, the senate had plenty of time to know and hate Domitian. Though he appointed many provincials to high office in Rome, Domitian ruled largely as an unabashed autocrat, which largely explains why the senate loathed him. (Domitian's habit of executing senators who objected too loudly accounts for the rest.) Feuding with the senate aside, Domitian was an efficient ruler. He spent more time campaigning than any emperor since Augustus. He established good relations with the army by marrying the daughter of Corbulo and leading the legions on a brief but successful attack on the Germans. Domitian's marriage was stable and successful but produced no heir, a development that had huge implications for the empire.

Although unpopular with the Roman elite, Domitian nevertheless completed the empire's recovery from Nero's abuses and the devastation of civil war. He helped this process by restoring the amount of silver in the Roman *denarius* which Nero had reduced to save money. The denarius was used to pay the army (which absorbed an estimated ninety percent of imperial revenue) so the wide distribution of better coinage had a dramatic effect on the economy. Regrettably the improvement was temporary.

Debasing the coinage became a favourite trick of cash-strapped emperors and eventually led to runaway inflation.

On the Danube frontier Domitian had to contend with restive Sarmatian and Dacian tribes and a revolt by a provincial governor, Saturninus. However most of the empire was at peace, and economic growth once again helped to bind Rome's empire into a unified economy with ever-strengthening cultural bonds. Domitian was eventually assassinated, a fate he had long feared and at which at least some senators had connived. The senate proclaimed Marcus Nerva as Caesar on the very same day, which suggests some degree of planning. Though the senate declared Domitian *damnatio memoriae* (in other words, his reign was to be officially forgotten), his legacy remained. Domitian had laid the foundations for prosperity to come, albeit a prosperity overseen by increasingly autocratic emperors.

Literature in the early empire

> No man's so brutish he can't be cultured / If he'll work patiently on self-improvement.
>
> Horace, *Epistles* 1.39–40

The greatest literature of Rome was written in the early empire and the preceding age of the dynasts. This at least was the opinion of those in the fifth century CE. Then, or soon after, books inscribed on papyrus were transferred to the more durable medium of parchment. This was crucially important: almost nothing not transcribed to parchment has survived other than as fragments. Parchment was enormously expensive, so even a very rich man had to choose which parts of his library he wished to preserve. The late imperial period's fascination with the first century means the literature of this period has survived, while other than church histories, the literature of later centuries generally has not.

What remains is the merest fraction of what was lost. By chance two novels, the *Satyricon* of Petronius Arbiter and *The Golden Ass* of Apuleius have (mostly) survived, while many similar works vanished without trace. Likewise we have the near-complete works of Tacitus but nothing of the *History of Flavianus*, written in the last days of the empire. Livy's story of Rome's rise to empire fascinated many late Romans, so this story has been preserved. However the later part of Livy's history tells of civil war and anarchy, phenomena with which later Romans were depressingly familiar and saw no need to preserve. Thanks to changing tastes today we would happily exchange much of what we have for that which was lost. Those who selected the books to transcribe to parchment were interested as much in style as in substance. Tacitus survived less because he was a great historian than because he wrote superb prose in the style known today as 'silver Latin'. The unadorned prose of Cato the Elder's *Origines* interested few, so only fragments survive of one of the first histories of ancient Rome.

Poetry

Roman poetry consciously drew on the legacy of ancient Greece, for in first-century Rome the fusion of Greek and Roman cultures was nearing completion. How deeply that combined culture was embedded in poetry of the empire becomes plain when we examine the first-century poets. Despite writing classical Graeco-Roman poetry, none of these poets were Greek and few were from Rome. Perhaps the greatest poet of the era was Virgil, from Mantua in Cisalpine Gaul. Born in about 70 BCE he was already middle-aged when Augustus seized power. Like all poets who were not personally wealthy, Virgil survived on the support of wealthy patrons. He soon came to the attention of Augustus, perhaps because his early poems, the *Eclogues*, described in all-too-moving detail the misery that land confiscations caused his homeland in the Veneto. Augustus' confidante Maecenas was an enthusiastic supporter of the arts. His patronage drew Virgil into the imperial circle and his poetry came to symbolise the new era in Rome. Yet Virgil eschewed contemporary issues. As Horace warned another friend and fellow poet, writing on near-contemporary events:

> You are crossing a field thick with hazards, Pollio.
> You are treading on fires merely banked beneath deceptive ash.

Horace, Odes 2.1.7–8

Virgil's greatest work is *The Aeneid*, which gives the retelling of the early legends of Rome a very Augustan twist. Readers are reminded that Iulus is the son of the protagonist Aeneas, the grandson of the goddess Venus and ancestor of Augustus. A constant in the poem is Rome's destiny and that the current unrest was the prelude to an age of tranquil prosperity. In Virgil's poetry, Rome's empire was both justified and divinely ordained. As one of Virgil's poetical characters proclaims:

> Your task, Roman, is to rule and bring to men the ways of government, to impose upon them the arts of peace, to spare those who submit and to subdue the arrogant.

Virgil, Aeneid 6.851–3

Interest in Virgil's poetry was intense even as it was written; Augustus would send messengers to badger the poet for progress reports. Virgil's reputation grew in the years after his death in 19 BCE. His poetry was a source of Roman pride, universally recognised as bringing the Latin language to the same sublime heights that Homer had taken his native Greek. For the rest of the imperial era Virgil was a staple of educational curricula;

cultured aristocrats larded their speech with Virgilian references, just as Virgil's contemporaries had quoted Homer.

Horace was another great non-Roman poet of the early first century. Five years younger than Virgil, he was born in Venusia in south-central Italy, in a town allegedly founded by one of the heroes of Virgil's *Aeneid*. Like Virgil, Horace was from relatively humble origins; his father was a freedman. Also like Virgil, Horace was embroiled in the troubles of his time. Mark Antony and Octavian trounced the army of Brutus in which Horace fought, causing the poet to flee for his life from the battlefield. The young man returned to Italy to find his small family estate confiscated. He found work as a clerk and in his leisure time wrote poetry. A none-too-flattering satire of Maecenas drew that man's attention and yet again, a potential voice of opposition was channelled into producing great poetry which implicitly backed the current regime.

Ovid was a minor Roman aristocrat. Though not born in Rome, he was educated there and held some junior administrative posts. He seems to have been friends with Horace but was barely on nodding terms with the shy and withdrawn Virgil. Some of Ovid's works are now lost, but his *Metamorphoses* and *Heroides* in themselves qualify him as a leading poet of the golden age of Latin literature. Today Ovid is probably best known for his scurrilous *Ars Amatoria* ('The art of love'); an ode to seduction Roman style, which instructs men and women, both married and unmarried, on how to conduct an amorous liaison. The *Ars Amatoria* offended Augustus, who combined the roles of strait-laced emperor and serial philanderer. Possibly because his verses struck too close to home, Ovid was exiled to Tomis on the shores of the Black Sea, where he remained until his death in 17 (or possibly 18) CE at the age of sixty.

Apart from this 'big three', the works of several contemporaries have survived. These include the elegies of Propertius and a few short poems by Sulpicia, a teenage poet who wrote to a lover under the nom de plume Cerinthus (*cerinthus* was literally the wax of the tablet on which the poem was written). Sulpicia's poems are included among the works of Tibullus, an elegiac poet who was also a friend of Horace.

History

> History illuminates truth and is the teacher of life.
>
> Cicero, *On the Orator* 2.9.36

Much of what we think we know of the history of early Rome was written some six centuries later. Today, there is considerable controversy about how far these histories are distorted by myth and propaganda and are anything but wholesale invention. However, so far, archaeological discoveries of earliest Rome are consistent with Roman legend. The Augustan historians wrote the early history of Rome to tell Romans who they were, partly fabricated though the image may have been. As new Roman citizens accumulated in their tens of thousands, such works acquainted Gauls, Spaniards and Syrians with the story of the nation they had joined.

Greeks are well represented in Roman historiography. Indeed, Rome's first historians probably wrote in Greek, imitating historians such as Thucydides and Xenophon, whom they had studied when young. Livy is known today exclusively for his monumental work *Ab Urbe Condita* ('from the foundation of the city'), although much of it is now lost. Like many writers of Latin's golden age, Livy's youth was marred by the civil wars that devastated much of the north Italian countryside where he grew up. Livy's work ardently supported the Roman Republic, something the new Augustan regime cheerfully accepted since it also claimed to support the Republic. Livy found favour partly because his text reflected the notorious prudishness of his home city of Patavium, which Augustus held should be the moral standard for the empire.

At times Livy used the earlier Greek historian Polybius so comprehensively that one can follow the texts line-by-line and note occasional mistranslations. However, he also had sources now lost to us, such as access to the senate record house, where he personally viewed the treaties and diplomatic reports that he described. Livy's version of the foundation of Rome has become the accepted legend. How far it reflects reality is passionately debated, as sources such as Plutarch's *Life of Romulus* show that different versions of the foundation of Rome remained in circulation almost a century later.

Dionysius of Halicarnassus was a contemporary of Livy, though never as famous. (It is said one man came to Rome from Gades in Spain simply to see Livy in the flesh and having done so returned home content that his trip had been worthwhile.) Dionysius was Greek and one of his objectives was to show that Rome had a Graeco-Roman culture from the outset. His *Roman Antiquitie*s is a study of Roman history and culture up to the first Punic war of 264 BCE. Only the first eleven of this twenty-book saga remain, though other excerpts have survived. While his love of rhetoric leads to speeches invented wholesale by the historian, Dionysius seems to have striven for authenticity; and as the rhetoric was admired by late antiquity and so preserved on parchment, modern historians cannot complain.

It is an oddity of Roman history that as we move further from the empire's foundation and nearer to our own time the evidence becomes scarcer and more unreliable. Writers of the Augustan age and later decades described the early imperial period in detail. Nevertheless the focus is mainly on the capital and the imperial court. The world outside the city of Rome is generally seen in terms of places that pay tax, rebel or are conquered. The major exception is a near-contemporary narrative set in an eastern client kingdom between the years 4 BCE and about 60 CE. Here the Romans make only incidental appearances which become more frequent as the different protagonists become involved with the senior authorities. This text is the New Testament. For most of the life of Jesus and in the travels of the apostles and St Paul, Rome and its empire form the backdrop against which people get on with their daily lives, their laws and culture largely undisturbed by Roman hegemony. Undoubtedly this also held true in Africa, Spain, Gaul and rural Italy. Fundamental change had begun, but would be noticeable only over decades and remain incomplete centuries later.

3
The golden age

Pax Aeterna, Felicitas Temporum. (Eternal peace, the happiness of the times.)

Legends on contemporary Roman coins

The century which followed the assassination of Domitian in 96 CE was famously praised by the historian Edward Gibbon:

> If a man were called to fix the period in the history of the world, during which the condition of the human race was most happy and prosperous, he would, without hesitation, name that which elapsed from the death of Domitian to the accession of Commodus. The vast extent of the Roman Empire was governed by absolute power, under the guidance of virtue and wisdom. The armies were restrained by the firm but gentle hand of four successive emperors, whose characters and authority commanded involuntary respect.

Gibbon, *The Decline and Fall of the Roman Empire* Vol. I Ch.3

Though the happiness of millions is always to be valued, even more important in the long run was the creation of a true Roman empire; that is, an empire *of* Romans rather than an empire ruled by Rome. Before 90 CE, if the Greeks or Spanish (for example) had had a viable chance of opting out of the empire, they probably would have done. By the end of the second century this was no longer true; the peoples of the empire mostly saw their aspirations in an imperial context. Rather than lead their tribe, top aristocrats in a Roman province dreamed of joining the Roman senate. Minor aristocrats strove for dominance in their local *civitas* and to achieve it used Roman social instruments, such as patronage and networks of useful 'friends' (*officia* and *amicitia*).

All aristocrats demonstrated their wealth by civic works, the giving of Roman-style games or the building of amphitheatres or chariot-racing courses (circuses) to house the games. In the provinces, there was a steady increase in Roman-style basilicas, baths and theatres, and tastes changed to match. The biographer Philostratus, in his *Life of Apollonius* (4.22), complained that the Athenians, never previously interested in the very Roman institution of gladiatorial games, 'now flock to watch the slaughter'. Aquincum (in modern Hungary) developed an extensive aqueduct system and Caesaraugusta (Zaragosa, in Spain) acquired a large theatre, where plays by Greek and Roman playwrights such as Sophocles and Plautus were performed.

The former tribes and city-states came to think of themselves as part of a larger whole. Farming was still a subsistence activity for many but, like the poet and craftsman, farmers had a larger market for their wares. An Italian maker of Arratine table pottery might work for a client in Africa by the light of a Gallic lamp while wearing a tunic of Amorgas cloth from the Greek Cyclades. His evening meal might include cheeses from Sicily, bread made from Egyptian wheat and the highly spiced Spanish fish relish, *garum*.

International economic integration led to a feeling of being part of a wider whole. This was encouraged by the Roman authorities, which permitted the relatively free movement of people and goods from province to province. Equally importantly, membership of the Roman army was open to provincials. Those with specialist skills, such as Syrian archers or Sarmatian cavalry, might serve anywhere from Germany to the Euphrates. Roman citizens from the provinces could join the legions, and many did, to the extent that, apart from the solidly Italian Praetorian Guard, the ancestors of most second-century legionaries had been defeated by the Roman army.

This does not mean that the empire became homogeneous. Some peoples – particularly the tribes of northern Britain and the Jews of Judea – bucked the integrationist trend and passionately sought independence. Furthermore, provincial Romans did not abandon their native culture; rather, they blended it with the Graeco-Roman model. Archaeology has shown that towns such as Atuatuca in Gallia Belgica had pottery, sculpture, town layout and religion similar to, but distinct from, comparable sites such as Dionysias (modern Suwayda) in Syria and Thugga/Dougga in Africa. Thugga/Dougga is an excellent example of a cultural synthesis that seamlessly integrated Numidian, Punic, Hellenistic and Roman elements into a unique whole. Furthermore, the empire was itself divided into the Latin west and the Greek east: a division that not only affected the future of the Roman Empire but that remains a real force in Europe two millennia later.

The Latin west

> To tell the truth, there are many parts of Italy in which no man puts on a toga until he is buried in it.
>
> Juvenal, *Satires* 3.171–2

Culturally and economically, the Latin west consisted of two parts: the Mediterranean regions of Italy, Spain, Africa and southern Gaul, and the rest of Gaul, Britain, Roman Germany and the Alpine and Danubian provinces.

Hispania, south-eastern Gaul and Africa, linked by maritime trade to Italy, were originally suppliers of raw materials and agricultural produce to the Italian market. As Cato the elder had famously demonstrated in the days of the Republic, when the winds were right, a fig picked in Africa could be eaten in Rome that same week. Thanks to bustling ports such as Puetoli in Italy, Carthage in Africa and Gades in Hispania, goods could circulate through the Mediterranean region in days. However, goods bound for the north-west of the empire by ox waggon through the Alps could take months to arrive. Gradually, exports became more sophisticated and inter-regional trade expanded. Archaeologically, this can be seen in manufactured products such as oil lamps. In the early period, these were generally of Italian provenance but by the second century CE were locally made or even exported to Italy. Ease of access by sea also encouraged wealthy Romans to acquire lands in the Mediterranean provinces; in later centuries much of the province of Africa was owned by Roman senators.

In Hispania, peace and imperial control of the silver mines led to efficient exploitation of the peninsula's mineral wealth. In his *Natural History* (33.78) Pliny the Elder reports twenty thousand pounds of gold were mined from Galicia, Asturias and Lusitania alone. The province also supplied the empire with most of its copper. This bounty led to prosperous towns and wealthy provincials, who became an important constituency in the Roman senate. The emperors Trajan and Hadrian were both born in the city of Italica in Hispania Baetica.

The north-west of the empire generally underwent greater social and cultural change than the Greek east or Italy, where urbanism had been common centuries or even millennia before. For the Greeks, and scarcely less for the Italians, the heroes of Homer and the Olympian gods were integral to their landscape and culture. Hercules, for example, had allegedly visited Evander on the site where Rome was later founded. In contrast, before their absorption into the empire, Britain and northern Gaul had known the Mediterranean world only through rare visits by traders and the occasional military incursion. The empire's north-west gradually began to import and adapt the legends and religion of the Mediterranean peoples. They did not replace local belief systems but fused with them, creating hundreds of regional variants on a common theme.

If trade integrated the Mediterranean provinces, the north-west was largely Romanised through the army. Britain generally housed three legions – II Augusta, XX Valeria Victrix and IX Hispana. (The latter famously vanishes from army records after around 120 CE, leading to modern speculation that it was destroyed by the Picts.) The legions in a province made their presence felt in a number of ways. First, although before 197 CE soldiers were forbidden to marry, many forged unofficial relationships in the towns (*canabae*) which inevitably formed around any permanent Roman camp. On discharge, these soldiers settled in the *canabae* and were an interface between the army and the local provincials. Many 'legionary towns' later became flourishing cities, for example, Leon in Spain, which takes its name from the legion (VII Gemina Felix) that was based there. Although only a small military force was actually stationed in Gaul, the Gauls were eager recruits to the Roman army and, if the epigraphic evidence of tombstones is a guide, contributed substantially to the manpower of the Rhineland and British armies.

The long-term presence of the legions strongly affected provincial economies. The army needed large amounts of foodstuffs – the British legions and auxilia alone consumed some fifty tonnes of meat and grain a day – and considerable amounts of pottery, iron and servants. Britain's mining industry developed partly to serve the needs of the legions; the surplus lead and tin were exported to Rome. The slag heaps in the Weald and Dean show that in the second century, Roman ironworking in Britain was large in scale. The mineral wealth of Britain, and later of Dacia, was exported to Gaul, as it became easier for Gallic metalworkers to import raw material rather than mine worked-out or less accessible local seams. Manufacturing in Gaul developed rapidly. Gallic craftsmanship was prized even before Gaul was integrated into the Roman Empire; the Roman legionary helmet, for example was based on a Gallic shape. During the second century, Gaul supplied textiles, glassware, ceramics and metalwork to much of the west. Mostly, this was the work of individual craftsmen, working with a few apprentices or labourers but there are signs that some businesses employed large numbers of workers in something like a factory system.

In Britain, Romanisation was less pronounced than in Gaul or Hispania. In Gaul some drinking vessels in local taverns carried Latin mottoes and second-century inscriptions reveal that the upper classes, at least, were bilingual. In Britain, the influence of Rome was strongest in the south-east and declined further west or north. Even in the south-east Romanisation was largely an urban phenomenon; most second-century Britons kept to their traditional culture, though the *Pax Romana* brought inter-tribal warfare to a halt. Scattered comments in written sources and surviving inscriptions show that Britons appear to have discovered a taste for litigation; matters once settled by duels or warfare were now decided by jurists and judges. Syncretism can also be seen in British religion: the Graeco-Roman gods were accepted but contained aspects of local deities. The addition of

Local aspects of divinity

An Olympian god had aspects: different sides to his divinity. Jupiter/Zeus was god of thunder but also of hospitality. In her aspect of Aphrodite/Venus Benetrix the goddess of love, protected marriage; but in her aspect of Aphrodite/Venus Porne, goddess of lust, she often undermined the same institution.

When the Britons adopted an Olympian god, they often created a new aspect of the god that resembled a local divinity. Thus, we find Graeco-Romano-British deities such as Minerva Sulis, where the local goddess Sulis became an aspect of Athena/Minerva. At Corbridge, Quintus Terentius Firmus made a dedication to Apollo in his aspect of Apollo Maponus. This dedication was not only made by a Roman but by the Prefect of the Camp of Legio VI Victrix. In other words, a very senior Roman officer accepted the conflation of what were originally different deities.

British aspects to Graeco-Roman gods shows that Romanisation worked both ways. Provincials become more Roman in ideology and self-image but their interpretation of what it meant to be Roman changed the outlook of the original Romans.

Britain

The Britons cheerfully put up with conscription, taxes and the other burdens of imperial rule; yet they will not tolerate oppression. They have become subjects, not slaves.

Tacitus, *Agricola* 1.13

One of the most striking remnants of second-century Roman Britain is the frontier structure of Hadrian's Wall. Perhaps the most significant feature of this wall – a very physical demonstration of the limits of Roman influence on the island – is that it was built at all. The Romans could have, and did, reach a lot further north. The Flavian general Agricola fought and won a major battle at Mons Graupius, in what is today northern Scotland. However, the Romans found no useful resources in the far north of Britain and by the second century were no longer interested in conquest for its own sake. Economically, it was cheaper to keep the northern tribes out than to try to subdue them.

The function of Hadrian's Wall and similar defences is often misconstrued as attempting to keep barbarians out of Roman lands. Some modern historians, recognising the impracticality of this have decided that frontier structures – *limes* in Roman parlance – were actually for controlling the flow of goods and little else. (Finding out exactly what happened at the borders of empire is today called 'Frontier Studies' and is practically an academic discipline in itself.) Hadrian's Wall artificially reproduced an effect similar to that of natural barriers such as the Rhine. Rivers and walls are generally ineffective at preventing large-scale military incursions. However, the point of incursions is to steal booty or livestock, which are both difficult to get over walls and rivers, while the same walls and rivers are very effective channels for mustering a force to meet and punish invaders as they return home. Furthermore, at points Hadrian's Wall runs along a cliff edge, an obstacle far more formidable than the wall above. The only reason for the wall in this area was to demonstrate to awed locals that Rome had huge resources and would use them to stay.

The Rhine and Danubian provinces

Upper and Lower Germany were Rome's most crucial frontier region. Until the end of the second century the Romans dreamed of conquering all Germany but in practice the frontier remained at the Rhine. A Germanic invasion from beyond the Rhine could reach Rome within a month, so seven or eight legions – a substantial part of the Roman army – were stationed in or near the Rhinelands.

The regular spacing of Roman farms in the Germanic provinces, almost up to the frontier, shows that in this region, Romanisation was a deliberate policy, implemented through settlement and (as we know from literary sources) the cultivation of local grandees. This, combined with economic development, brought increased prosperity and population growth. The density of archaeological remains suggests that the second century population of the Rhineland provinces was higher than any before the modern era. The Danube provinces were frequently raided during the first century, ultimately provoking one of the last great Roman conquests: the conquest of Dacia. Though imperial rule was relatively brief, Dacia was sufficiently Romanised to acquire its modern name of Romania and a language that is very close to Latin.

From an empire ruled by Rome to an empire of Romans

The second century accelerated the process by which conquered peoples were integrated into the empire. What we call 'Romanisation' did not mean that conquered peoples abandoned their traditions for those of the Romans but rather described a process of fusion and adaptation through which cultures and peoples adjusted to becoming part of a larger whole.

The colonies of the first century became substantial towns, many of which continued to thrive long after the fall of the Roman Empire; today Cologne (Colonia Agrippinenis), Mainz (Mogontiacum), Strasbourg (Argentoratum) and Augsburg (Augusta Vindelicorum) are examples from just one region. Augusta Vindelicorum is also an example of Rome's deliberate policy of transforming native tribes into *civitates*. The tribe of the Vindelici lived at the important junction of the Rhine and Danube provinces, on a passage through the eastern Alps to the Danube. Augusta Vindelicorum was created there, and became the most important city in the province of Rhaetia. It was a focus both for the Romanisation of the region and the aspirations of the local elite. Other towns in this area, such as Kempten, had more substantial public buildings than their population appears to warrant, which suggests they were built as manifestations of the civic structure that Rome was attempting to impose.

There had been a Roman presence south and west of the Danube since the third century BCE but the peoples of what became Dalmatia, Upper and Lower Pannonia, and Upper and Lower Moesia fought hard against absorption into the empire. During the first century Tiberius fought several brutal campaigns in the region and a Pannonian rebellion deprived the Rhineland of the essential leadership and manpower that could have forestalled the Varian disaster of 9 CE. Given the crucial importance of the Danubian provinces to the integrity of the northern Roman frontier, it is unsurprising that they generally contained more than six legions, together with a considerable number of auxiliaries. Archaeologically, the record shows an interesting fusion of cultures, with local gods becoming aspects of their closest Roman equivalent, such as Mercury Naissus and Neptune Ovianus. Mars acquired aspects from several local war gods, becoming Mars Bedaius and Mars Celeia.

Tombstones of local grandees show them wearing Roman togas or tunics, while their wives remain in native dress. Pottery and metalwork continued to be made in the distinctive local tradition. Danubian metalwork became popular with the Roman army; belt buckles and cloak clasps in this style are found in former legionary bases across Europe. There is also epigraphic evidence that, in the Danubian provinces, contrary to their conventional practice, the Romans did not try to link *civitas* (tribe) with *municipium* (town). Undoubtedly this was because the tribal structure was useful for the recruitment of auxilia and later, as ex-auxiliaries became citizens, their descendants became valued recruits to the legions. Tombstones again reflect this process, with the distinctly non-Roman names of first century soldiers gradually replaced by the standard Roman *tria nomina* ('three names') such as Titus Valerius Pudens, a Pannonian legionary whose tombstone is now in the British Museum.

A crucial artery of empire ran just south of the Danube provinces. This, the *via Egnatia*, was Rome's only connection with the eastern empire during the *mare clusum* ('closed sea') when the Mediterranean winter prevented sailing. From the main trunk of the *via Egnatia*, smaller roads led off to the north-east and along the Roman frontier along the Danube. The main function of these roads was to allow the legions to be deployed rapidly but they also helped commerce to expand. Wealth flowed back to Italy along the *via Egnatia*; some grain was grown for export, especially in Moesia, and Danubian timber has been found in buildings along the Mediterranean shore. Mining was also developed, again partly to serve the needs of the legions. Iron and silver were mined in considerable quantities and the conquest of Dacia allowed the region's famous gold mines to fill the imperial coffers. The growing prosperity of the north-western provinces meant that in the second century, northern Italy surpassed the south and centre of the peninsula in wealth and commercial activity; a lead that it has never relinquished.

The Greek east

For years now the Orontes [a river in Lebanon and Syria] has been disgorging into the Tiber.

A character of Juvenal's complains about immigrants
in *Satires* 3.62

Where Rome brought a new, urban and cosmopolitan perspective to the north and north-west of Europe, its cultural impact on the peoples of the east was less dramatic. There, urban culture had been established for millennia and patterns of international trade were long established. Also, while the Latin language unified the diverse peoples of the west, the east already had common tongues in Greek and Syriac; Latin was mainly a language of officialdom.

The main effect of the Roman Empire in the east was felt through the *Pax Romana*, which brought economic growth and prosperity to the western seaboard of Anatolia and cities such as Alexandria in Egypt.

Greece had perhaps contributed most to Mediterranean culture in the millennium before 100 CE. Its culture had spread as far as modern Afghanistan and fused with Roman culture on Europe's most westerly shores, but in the second century CE the land where it started was a peaceful imperial backwater. The Romans were sentimental about Greece; emperors as diverse as Nero and Hadrian were passionate philhellenes. Consequently, much of Achaea (as the province was called) consisted of 'free' cities that paid little or no tax to Rome, although many Achaean cities were too poor to have contributed much even if they had been taxed. The emperor Hadrian attempted to unite Greek cities into a loose social and religious union, the 'Panhellenion', but once his successors lost interest it, like most previous Greek political unions, collapsed in infighting.

If the situation warranted it, the emperors had little compunction about interfering in the affairs of cities, 'free' or not. Generally, such interference took the form of a special official, who held the self-explanatory title of 'corrector'. Even Athens merited the visit of a corrector sent by Trajan to sort out a deep financial crisis. Athens held an honoured place in Roman culture and many Romans went to Attica to study. One such was the writer and grammarian Aulus Gellius (approximately 125–182 CE), who published his notes and musings from his time as a student in Athens as the *Attic Nights*. We also know much about the contemporary city from the sophist and senator Herodes Atticus, who rose to high rank in the imperial system under Hadrian. Herodes added to Athens a small theatre for poetry readings and drama and a stadium for sporting events. The emperors Antoninus Pius and Marcus Aurelius boosted the city's academic reputation by establishing a school of rhetoric. Today, the flourishing of

Greek writers in this period is often referred to as the 'second sophistic' movement. While Athens polished its reputation for learning and the arts, its former great rival, Sparta, became so Spartan as to become virtually a parody of itself. The *agoge*, a sadistic method of raising young men to be impervious to pain and discomfort, had once created the city's invincible warrior, the *hoplites*. Now, Roman tourists lined specially built stands, wincing as they watched particularly dramatic rites of passage.

Contemporary authors, such as Pausanias, depict the Peloponnese as a land dotted with ruined cities and once-thriving farms abandoned for richer pastures elsewhere in the empire. (This bleak picture has been mitigated by archaeology which has shown that some areas and towns continued to thrive.) Nevertheless, the biographer Plutarch, who stubbornly stayed on in the ancient city of Chaeronea, remarked 'this is a small town and I remain here to stop it getting any smaller'. Corinth, perhaps the most prosperous city in early Greece, was wiped off the map by Rome in 146 BCE. The sack of Corinth horrified the Mediterranean world; for almost a century, one of the most famous and cultured cities of antiquity was a lifeless ruin. It was refounded as a Roman colony by Julius Caesar; its strategic position on the isthmus brought rapid prosperity. Second-century Corinth was the commercial centre of the province and the city's traditional Isthmian games were a tourist attraction second only to the Olympics. The emperor Antoninus Pius made the region to the north-west of the Peloponnese into a separate province, Epirus. It is uncertain why he made this administrative change but it established a trend for more and smaller provinces that accelerated in later centuries.

Macedonia and Thrace had fiercely resisted assimilation into the Roman Empire, yet by the second century both were stable imperial provinces. As in most of the empire, Romanisation occurred but archaeology shows that both regions maintained their distinctive language and culture, especially away from the larger cities. The Thracians had been exposed to Greek culture for much longer than the Gauls or Iberians, and indeed had made a significant contribution to that culture. Nevertheless, the Thracians maintained a separate identity: urbanism was less established in Thrace than elsewhere in the empire and the army (another instrument of Romanisation) was largely based in Moesia to the north. The Romans attempted, through reduced taxes, to attract inhabitants to new towns but most Thracians remained on the land, in their tribal villages.

Asia Minor

Across the Hellespont, the land mass of Anatolia contained a fascinating mix of peoples and cultures. Civilisation here was ancient: the Hittite, Assyrian, Persian and Seleucid empires had risen and fallen long before the Roman Empire conquered the region. The conquest was not easy; it took more than a century for the cities and towns of the Anatolian seaboard to recover their pre-conquest prosperity.

Roman government in Asia Minor followed the conventional pattern of dividing provinces into largely autonomous administrative districts. However, there was variation, in that some districts appear to have been run by priests of the regional cults, a relic of the times when places such as Comana were largely run by priests of Ma, the moon goddess. Cities such as Ephesus, on the western coast, were major trading centres that shipped goods westward from the famed Silk Road and in exchange, moved Roman gold east. In 1976, a fragmentary inscription was discovered at Ephesus, which though occasionally ambiguous and hard to interpret, gives a reasonably clear picture of the customs duties and imperial levies on goods entering and leaving the province. There were few barriers to trade other than banditry (impossible to stamp out in the rugged Anatolian interior) and tolls (which the Romans imposed at the borders of most jurisdictions). Ports such as Sinope were made wealthy by the exploitation of the extensive fish stocks of the Euxine and by re-exporting the rich grain crops of the Bosporan region.

The terrain of Asia Minor is not conductive to easy travel; as a result, each area retained a distinctive cultural identity. Second-century Galatians (for example) retained Gallic elements in their culture, despite having dwelt in the highlands of Anatolia for the previous four hundred years. Indeed, even in the fifth century CE we know, from the commentaries of St Jerome, that the Galatians spoke a variant of Gallic. However, epigraphic evidence suggests that Greek was increasingly preferred to the plethora of ancient languages peculiar to districts and valleys. (Pontus alone was said to have sixty languages.) Most educated Asians were probably bilingual in Greek and their local language.

We know a lot about the administration of Pontus and the neighbouring former kingdom of Bithynia in Asia Minor. On assimilation by Rome, the two kingdoms had been combined into a single senatorial province. In the early second century, this province was governed by Pliny the Younger. The good-natured Pliny was an indefatigable correspondent and well over a hundred of his letters have survived. These give a good – if idealised – picture of the life of a senior aristocrat. As provincial governor, Pliny wrote frequently to the emperor Trajan (who reigned from 98–117 CE) about the governance of his province. Pliny was apparently selected as governor because of his legal background; extravagant spending had led to disarrayed finances in the cities and Pliny's immediate task was to sort things out. Trajan wrote:

> I persuade myself that the people of the province will be convinced that I pay close attention to their best interests. You will act toward them in such a way that it should be obvious that I could have chosen no better person to represent me.

Trajan in *Pliny's Letters to Trajan* 10.17

Pliny expected Trajan to manage affairs to a remarkable extent. Issues such as whether public slaves should serve as prison guards were not sorted out by the man on the spot but were referred to Rome. Closer examination of such issues shows that they were those that might lead a suspicious emperor to believe his subordinate was plotting treason. Regarding the prison guards, Pliny would have known that any paramilitary organisation made the emperor uneasy; Augustus once executed a man for organising the Roman fire brigade too efficiently. In another example, an escaped slave appealed for sanctuary while clinging to the emperor's statue; Pliny was at pains to avoid *lese-majest* in the matter. Another interesting case involved the ashes of two deceased aristocrats which were placed in a room that contained a statue of the emperor. Pliny, as was his wont, asked Trajan whether this constituted disrespect for the emperor. The sensible reply was:

> My dearest Secundus, you know very well that it is my standing policy not to intimidate people by severe and rigorous measures with regard to my person. Nor should we take every slight offence as an act of treason.

> Trajan in *Pliny's Letters to Trajan* 10.86

Trajan's replies are usually brief and to the point, albeit wrapped by standard polite expressions at the head and foot. One can imagine a busy emperor, dealing with a mass of correspondence from all over the empire, replying in a few terse words that secretarial staff fleshed out into complete letters. When Pliny wrote to inform the emperor that dedications and vows had been taken for his health and well-being, Trajan replied:

> My dearest Secundus, I received the satisfaction of being informed by your letter that you, together with the people whom you govern, have discharged and renewed your vows to the immortal gods for my health and happiness.

> Trajan in *Pliny's Letters to Trajan* 10.45

This is probably a standard response, given all imperial officials under the same circumstances. Both letter and response were probably laid before the emperor for no more than a quick signature. Such correspondence flowed steadily back and forth between the imperial palace and the far corners of the empire, using an imperial postal system set up for the purpose. Pontus in Asia Minor needed this postal system less than most provinces, because even in the relatively tranquil second century an emperor's first concern was for military matters. Asia Minor flourished precisely because there was little military activity. When we hear of the army it is either because Pliny wants specialists from the army for civil engineering projects or needs to post small legionary garrisons to troublespots:

> Sir, you acted with your usual agreeable prudence and foresight when you ordered the illustrious Calpurnius Macer to send a legionary centurion [and his guard] to Byzantium. Could you also consider the city of Juliopolis as deserving the same favour?

Trajan in *Pliny's Letters to Trajan* 10.81

In this case Trajan refused. His correspondence shows a reluctance to disperse the legions unless absolutely necessary. We see also in his letter a comment that if legionaries misbehave, this should be documented and the miscreants sent to their officers for discipline. Even in a settled province the army was privileged; by and large soldiers were not subject to civil law and misdeeds were handled internally.

The Middle East

If the Roman Empire in Asia Minor was more Greek than Roman, and if Hellenistic influences were lightly felt in the countryside of Asia Minor, local cultures were more established

in the Middle East. Here, Semitic peoples such as the Phoeni-
cians and the Jews had traded and fought with each other for
millennia. The province of Syria included the city of Damascus,
three thousand years old before Rome was founded and today
generally considered the world's oldest continuously inhabited
city. Tradition was strong and deep-rooted.

Syria was among the largest and most important provinces of
the empire; the governorship of Syria was one of the most prized
offices a Roman senator could hold. Emperors selected candidates with care, for, bordering the Parthian Empire, Syria had a
legionary presence that matched that of the Rhine and Danube
frontiers. The Euphrates River, on Syria's border, generally
marked the eastern limit of Roman power. This changed briefly
after Trajan's successful war in 106 CE, after which a new province, Mesopotamia, was formed east of the river. Trajan's successor Hadrian abandoned most of this province but retained part,
to establish Rome's dominance over the trading city of Palmyra.
Archaeology shows that Rome worked hard to maintain the *Pax
Romana* behind the frontiers. The road system was extended in
111–114 CE, when Trajan built a road through Arabia 'from Syria
to the Red Sea'. The remains of forts along the frontiers and at
key stopping-points along the trade routes show that a considerable body of auxiliary soldiers helped to keep the peace.

Local client kingdoms of the Republic (such as Nabataea)
had largely been absorbed into the formal structure of the
empire. However, one such state – the province of Judea –
never accepted the loss of its independence. An earlier rebellion
ended in 70 CE, when the armies of Vespasian and his son Titus
destroyed Jerusalem. When Vespasian used the military power
and prestige gained from crushing the Jewish rebellion to make
himself emperor, the support of Mucianus, governor of Syria, was
crucial to his success.

The defeat in 70 CE suppressed Jewish nationalism for
generations, partly because it left large tracts of Judea extensively

depopulated. The emperor Hadrian later proposed rebuilding Jerusalem, which had never fully recovered from the attentions of Titus and his legions. Hadrian was initially sympathetic to the Jews, though he antagonised them by banning circumcision, which, like many with Hellenistic views, he regarded as ritual mutilation. Jewish delight at the rebuilding of Jerusalem turned to dismay when Hadrian's architects unveiled a Hellenistic city, to be called Aelia Capitolina.

In 132 CE, a carefully planned uprising took place. It was led by Simon bar Kokhba, after whom the revolt is generally named. For the two and a half years of the rebellion Judea was independent. Once Judea was reconquered, a vindictive Hadrian and a massive Roman army tried hard to destroy Judaism altogether. At least half a million Jews were killed and their faith was banned. Aelia Capitolina (Jerusalem) was settled by legionaries and Jews were banned from the city. To further dissociate the people from their land, the province was thereafter called Syria Palestina. The name may be a corruption of the word 'Philistine', a people the Romans knew to be ancient enemies of the Jews. The effects of the bar Kokhba rebellion are still felt today, both in modern Judaism and the politics of the Middle East.

Jews and Christians

Many Jews believed bar Kokhba was the Messiah. This further alienated the relatively small but growing Christian faith which was already moving away from Judaism, for Christians believed that the Messiah had already lived. Jews and Christians were diffused throughout the empire but Christianity was international, while Judaism remained focused on the land of Israel. Christianity had been seen as a version of the Judaic faith but the bar Kokhba rebellion sharply differentiated nationalistic Jews from Christians. This widened the schism and caused members of each religion to consider themselves as being of separate faiths.

Egypt

The Judean rebellion affected the substantial populations of Jews elsewhere in the empire. The Jews of Alexandria had been numerous and influential, albeit generally at odds with the Hellenistic element, which used the rebellion as an excuse for a pogrom. Alexandria itself, a city founded by the Hellenic Alexander the Great, was the centre of Graeco-Roman culture in Egypt, although the Greek aspect greatly predominated over the Roman. However, the rest of Egypt was not neglected, because the annual flooding of the Nile produced the rich crops essential to the corn supply of Rome. Hadrian visited Egypt in the 120s CE; while he was there, the love of his life, a young man called Antinous, died in mysterious circumstances in the Nile. The grieving emperor established a city in his lover's memory and the special privileges he offered induced many – especially from the nearby town of Naucratis – to take up residence.

In Egypt, papyrus was used for documents both of official importance and casual notes. Many of these have been preserved in Egypt's dry sands and rubbish dumps, yielding a wealth of information on the day-to-day lives of ordinary Egyptians; information that is totally lacking in climates where such evidence rots. It is frustrating that the special position of Egypt means that much of the social and legislative structure described in these documents cannot be extrapolated to describe daily life and administrative systems in the rest of the empire. It is clear that, in Egypt, as elsewhere, Roman authority stayed in the background. For most native Egyptians, the Roman Empire was felt mainly through the presence of the army and the fact that this army enforced centuries of peace, broken only by frequent riots between Jews, Greeks and natives in Alexandria.

The army

> The village weavers are collectively to supply the required
> items [of clothing] ... all of pure, unstained wool, with properly
> finished hems.

> Army requisition in Cappadocia, circa 138 CE
> (*Selected papyri* 395)

It is often said that the Roman army of 100 CE represents the
peak of Roman military efficiency. A rival school of thought
claims that the Roman army of the late imperial era was at least
as well equipped and professional. However, whatever the quality of individual soldiers and units in late antiquity, the overall
efficiency of the army had diminished. For an army, logistics are
as important as individual military prowess; a second century
legionary could count on regular rations and pay. Equally
important, he could be replaced should he fall in battle, for
in the second century (unlike the fourth) membership of the
army was considered a privilege and there was no shortage of
recruits.

The second-century legions were restricted to Roman citizens of good character. Pliny mentions to Trajan that he discovered two slaves trying to enter the army, for which the punishment
was probably death. Recruits had to be a certain height and have
no physical deformities. Even then, they might need also a letter
of recommendation, preferably from a local magistrate or former
legionary.

Training was rigorous and involved hours of drill and practice
with the *rudis*, a wooden sword made deliberately heavier than
the real thing, the better to build up the muscles of a recruit's
sword arm. Even fully-fledged legionaries spent much of their
time practising drill and (in theory), any legion was able to drop
everything and march into battle at a moment's notice.

The rank structure of the legions differed from a modern army, as legionaries had no promotion ladder; most who signed on as legionaries remained so. There were different positions within the legionary structure; *munifex* being the lowest and *optio* the highest but these were appointments, rather than ranks. An *immunis* was a soldier with specialist skills, such as a clerk or a blacksmith. Though spared some of the more onerous duties of their fellow soldiers, the *immunes* did not outrank them. The rank of centurion was, very rarely, won by a legionary for exemplary conduct in battle but generally, this rank was purchased by the exchange of favours before the centurion joined the army. Although centurions might rise through the various graduations of the position, few were promoted beyond it. One such promotion might be to *praefectus castrorum*: prefect of the camp. The prefect oversaw the day-to-day running of a legionary camp and was generally only answerable to the legate, who ran the legion. The legionary legate was a political appointee; indeed, he could hardly be anything but, since even a single legion represented a significant part of the empire's military force.

Rome maintained some 300,000 men under arms. Although this represented about ninety percent of the imperial expenditure in any year, it was still a tiny force to police and defend an empire that stretched from the Thames to the Tigris. It worked only because the Romans had effective strategies for the economic projection of force and because the legionaries and their commanders were superb at their jobs. There was no official training for a Roman military commander but every senator was expected to be able to command a legion if necessary. A surviving document from the start of this era, the *Stratagems* of Frontinus, is a collection of military anecdotes, tactics, command and dirty tricks, collected by Frontinus for his edification before he took command of the legions in Britain.

Many young aristocrats served in the army as military tribunes and learned the working of the camp and command structure at first hand. However this era also saw the rise of the professional military tribune, for whom the army was a full-time career. Such men often commanded the auxiliary units that were an essential adjunct to the legions. Though more lightly armed than the legionaries, a standard auxiliary soldier would count as a heavy infantryman in most contemporary armies. Indeed, entire battles could be and were won by the auxilia alone. Unlike the legions, the auxilia were open to non-citizens. Since an honourable discharge after service of twenty years in the auxilia came with a diploma granting Roman citizenship, the auxilia were an instrument of Romanisation in many provinces.

Some auxiliary units, such as the Thracian cavalry and Syrian archers, were specialists who saw service all over the empire. Their tombstones have been found in York in the north of England and on the borders of Arabia. However, most units were recruited and served locally. This was because the particular skills of native auxiliary units were mainly useful in their native terrain: Numidian light cavalry, for example, were superb in open desert but for the forests and marshes of Germany the Romans needed units such as the Batavi, with their legendary ability to cross rivers at speed. Furthermore, the auxilia's native knowledge of people and terrain was invaluable to a legionary commander who might have arrived only weeks before.

The second century is generally considered a period of peace but there was hard fighting on several fronts. It took a massive army to crush the bar Kokhba revolt in Judea; in the generation before, the army under Trajan was by no means idle, for under Trajan, the Roman Empire reached its greatest extent. Paradoxically, for preceding eras we have detailed accounts of campaigns but only a few glimpses of the armour and appearance of the soldiers. For Trajan, we have only the rudimentary details of his campaigns, yet a very clear picture of his army in operation. This is because Trajan immortalised the army of his Dacian conquest on a column placed in the centre of Rome. This column (which was also Trajan's tombstone) has survived to the present day. It shows legionaries assaulting enemy fortifications, crossing rivers and being addressed by the emperor. Reconstructing the conquest of Dacia from the pictorial narrative of the column is tricky, because the column is as much about showing the emperor's relationship with the army as it is about the actual events.

We know that from the time of Domitian, in the late first century, the Dacian and Sarmatian people threatened the Danube frontier. Large-scale raids escalated into small wars, so as soon as he could, Trajan took the war to Dacia. The Dacians were no uncivilised barbarians; they had been exposed to Greek culture for longer than the Romans themselves and their cities had sophisticated fortifications. It is generally believed that King Decebalus united the different factions of Dacia, after which the Dacians abandoned their usual internecine warfare and became a threat to the empire's northern frontier.

Figure 3 The emperor Trajan addresses troops during the Dacian war. The variety of dress and armour on display might signify different units, or simply reflect the fact that Roman soldiers were less uniformly dressed than armies today. (Picture courtesy of Adrian Goldsworthy)

Thanks to Trajan's column, we have at least an idea of events in Dacia. However, Trajan's Parthian campaign of 116–117 CE is almost completely undocumented. We know only that Trajan advanced through Armenia and Mesopotamia as far as the Persian Gulf. This made the River Tigris the eastern frontier of the empire and created the new provinces of Assyria and Mesopotamia. The Parthian people were successors to the Hellenistic Seleucid kingdom of the east, which once had extended Mediterranean culture as far as the Himalayas. The Parthians had a unique culture, which is only now being uncovered but also maintained Hellenic culture (indeed entire Greek cities) and later gave refuge to Jews fleeing the persecution of Hadrian. The assaults of Trajan, and of his successors over the next century, crippled the Parthian empire, which never had Rome's military resources. Parthia's eventual fall did not bring peace to the east, for soon afterwards the militaristic and organised Sassanian Persian Empire arose to become an even greater threat.

Roman armies still employed two strategies from the early empire: economy of force and massively disproportionate retaliation. It took a lot to provoke the legions into action, because they were generally needed elsewhere. When they did act, it was to ensure that they would never have to return, sometimes by leaving no one to return to. Because they delivered so effectively on their threats, legions such as III Augusta in Africa and VIII Augusta in Argentoratum (Strasbourg) went decades without seeing significant action.

Legions could be positioned to hold more than one region or confront several threats simultaneously. In the 120s CE, III Cyrenica was one such multitasking legion. It moved from its long-term base in Alexandria to Bostra, which had been refounded by Trajan as the capital of Roman Arabia; the legion stamp of army builders appears on local roads, city gates and the amphitheatre. The soldiers clamped down on the smugglers for which the region was notorious and at the same time were a strategic reserve against a Parthian attack or a Jewish revolt. The disadvantage of having one legion confronting several threats was that it could only deal with one at a time. This was not a major problem in the peaceful era of the Antonines but it became so later, when legions desperately needed on one section of frontier were defending another or (as became ever more frequent) participating in a civil war.

Christianity

In a famous letter to Trajan (*Pliny's Letters to Trajan* 10.96), Pliny wrote:

> Because I've never been involved with a formal investigation of Christians, I'm not sure what the usual punishments are for them. Nor am I sure when an investigation should be started or how far one should go with it. ... For the present, my approach is as follows. If anyone is brought to me as an accused Christian, I personally ask if this were so. If the person admits it, I ask again and yet again, with a warning of what the accused faces if he admit it. Those who persist, I order to be taken off for execution, basically because no matter what they are admitting to, their pernicious obstinacy should not go unpunished. Some of these same fanatics are Romans so I have sent them to that city [Rome] for trial.

Pliny decided to investigate further. He did this by interviewing two ex-Christians who had recanted and by torturing two female Christian 'ministers' who were also slaves:

> The whole of their guilt or error was no more than that they met regularly before dawn on a certain day to chant hymns to Christ as though he were a god ... After completing this foolishness they would come together later for a meal of some common and innocuous food.

'Common and innocuous food' might indirectly refer to the veracity of the popular belief that Christians ate human flesh. In fact, Pliny's investigations found nothing 'but a sort of degenerate superstition' from which he felt many would recant, given the correct incentive. Trajan endorsed Pliny's approach. He added that no one should be charged on the basis of anonymous accusations, as this 'would set a bad example and is not in the spirit of our era':

> These people should not be hunted down but if they are charged before you and the charge is proven, they must be punished. But if anyone denies he is a Christian ... he must be acquitted on the basis of that recantation, however suspicious his former conduct.
>
> Pliny's Letters to Trajan Book 10

This was not the first time that Christians had come to the attention of the imperial authorities. The first time, of course, was Jesus' appearance before Pontius Pilate. Thereafter, the preaching of men such as St Peter and St Paul had sometimes provoked a degree of unrest. It seems that St Paul had a rough time in parts of Asia Minor; in 1 Corinthians 15:32 he wrote: 'we fought with wild beasts at Ephesus'.

By the time of Nero, in the 60s CE, there was an established Christian presence in Rome. Contemporary Romans considered Christianity an offshoot of Judaism and after Pompey captured Jerusalem in 63 BCE the population of Jews in Rome was numbered in the thousands. Christians themselves were uncertain how Jewish they were; the original church had multiple identities and frequent schisms. Many of the basic tenets of modern Christianity – the Trinity, the divinity of Jesus, the nature of sin – were hotly debated and did not become established dogma almost until the end of the Roman Empire itself.

Normally the Romans were easy-going about religion. If they particularly liked a deity, they adopted it, such as the Magna Mater ('Great Mother') from Asia Minor or Isis from Egypt. Gods

Did Christians burn Rome?

One 'Christian' sect may have consisted of violently nationalistic Jews who believed that their Messiah intended them to destroy Rome and liberate the holy land. If so, then there may be some truth to claims that this concept of Christianity led to religious terrorism and the burning of much of Rome in 64 CE, although it is probable the fire was a random disaster, or a deliberate act by Nero, which is highly improbable. After the fire, Christians were seized and 'confessed'. It is not clear whether they confessed to their faith or to burning down Rome but Nero used this excuse to launch the first of what was to be a sporadic series of official persecutions over the next two and a half centuries.

from other cultures were linked with the Olympian deities by syncretism. Other foreign gods were worshipped without either official sanction or persecution. There were Semitic followers of various versions of Baal across the empire who were persecuted only when Christianity became the dominant religion and the god Baal Zebul or 'Lord Prince' became in Christian eyes Beelzebub, the devil.

Rome was less tolerant of Christians in part because Christians were intolerant of any other religion. Roman gods were gods of the people as a whole and of each community in particular. The gods lived with the people in their temples, as 'super-patrons' of the cities that they blessed and protected with their presence. The temples of the gods were no more open to the public than are the private quarters of a modern mayor. And as with a modern mayor, neither love nor belief in his existence was required. Excessive devotion to a god was considered *superstitio* 'superstition'. The essential requirement of ancient gods (and modern mayors) was that citizens should pay their dues.

For a Roman god, those dues meant attending ceremonies in his honour and participating at sacrifices at his altar. (Roman altars were outside the temples.) Private belief was unnecessary but nor should a god be publicly repudiated, because the god in turn might repudiate the city, leaving it cursed and defenceless. Public unease about Christianity was felt precisely because Christians repudiated the *pax deorum*. It was not the worship of Christ that Romans objected to but the loud denouncement of those gods as demons or fallacies. In short, Christians were persecuted less for their religion than for vandalising the underpinnings of Roman civic life.

It is uncertain how many practising Christians there were in Pliny's time. Pliny himself remarked: 'Not just the city but villages and the countryside have also been infected by this perverse superstition' and claimed that in some places the altars of the old gods had been almost entirely abandoned. However, this letter of Pliny, and the texts of Josephus that mention Christianity in the early empire, were mainly preserved by monks, giving rise to the suspicion that the texts may have been adapted to reflect the views of those doing the preserving. It is certain that there were Christians at all levels of second-century society, from the lowest slave to the highest aristocrat. While impinging little on the official record, the religion continued to grow. Doctrinal issues were slowly resolved, although a coherent theology developed only after Christianity became the official religion of the Empire.

Roman pastimes

Romans are controlled by two things – subsidised grain and public spectacles. Political support depends as much on entertainments as on matters of state. Neglect of serious issues damages the state but neglecting entertainments causes harmful personal unpopularity.

Fronto, *Elements of History* 18

Most tasks in Roman society relied on manpower. Despite this, modern research has concluded that the average citizen did not work particularly hard. Most inhabitants of the Roman Empire were peasant farmers; while their work was back-breakingly hard at times, at others almost no work was required. (This is why in earlier times Roman peasants could take the summer off to conquer the world.) Furthermore, in some jobs, participation was unprofitable for citizens, due to the ubiquity of slaves who worked for free or at minimal cost. The workload of slaves varied enormously, from wretches used as beasts of burden in the fields and the mines, to favoured attendants of the aristocracy who were often better off than the common citizen.

In towns, the Roman day was divided into twelve hours of day and twelve of night. Because days were longer in summer and shorter in winter, day and night hours were never the same length except at the equinoxes. This was not a problem for sundials (the main form of time-keeping) but considerable effort was needed to make items such as water-clocks reflect this. Romans arose just before dawn and the Roman working day began. It usually ended six or seven hours later at the 'ninth hour'. (After which time prostitutes were allowed to practice, hence their nickname of 'ninth hour girls'.) This was early to mid-afternoon, at which time a Roman would enjoy a light lunch and a nap, before going to the bath-house to wash themselves before supper. In Rome, and most large towns, baths were impressive structures that were leisure centre, swimming pool and sauna combined; entry was free or only a minimal fee. Men and women might bathe together or separately, depending on local custom; separately was normal.

The importance of baths in Roman culture is reflected in the energy and expense that local authorities put into building and maintaining them. In Rome, baths were sponsored by the emperor himself and generally named after their builder. Trajan contributed spectacular baths, while, as the poet Martial remarked

Figure 4 The baths of Caracalla. Originally conceived by the emperor Septimius Severus and completed by his son around 216 CE, the baths are an impressive propaganda statement of the wealth of the regime. The design was the inspiration for Pennsylvania Station in New York. (Picture courtesy of Adrian Goldsworthy)

'What was worse than Nero? What is better than his baths?' Later the emperor Caracalla (209–217 CE) built baths which, even as ruins, remain highly impressive. As well as providing physical cleanness, exercise and probably a light massage, the baths were where many Romans met socially, often as a prelude to dining together. At a normal dinner the head of the family (the *paterfamilias*) might sit at table with his wife and children, and in poorer households with his slaves as well. However, for many Romans dining was more than the consumption of food. Communal and guild banquets were common and individual Romans liked to host dinner parties as often as their means permitted.

A Roman dinner party ideally had more than three and fewer than ten guests. Dinner parties were generally for men only (women gathered in morning *salons*), though the host's wife might make an appearance. At a dinner party, the guests were propped up on pillows, reclining two or three to a couch. They ate using one hand, enjoying dishes that were generally highly spiced finger food. Entertainment might be anything from poetry readings to gladiators or dancing girls, but the main purpose of the meal was conversation, which might range from philosophical discussion to business, bawdy stories or political intrigue. The host of a dinner party might bring a parasite picked up in the toilets. Roman toilets were communal affairs, in which users sat side by side on wooden benches and exchanged greetings and gossip during the proceedings. A *parasitos* (one who dies at another's expense) was a professional dinner guest, invited because of his passing fame, reputation for wit or knowledge of philosophy. The poet Martial was an eager parasite and boasts on occasion '*cena capta*' (dinner bagged). He remarks bitterly that a rival spent all day hanging around the public toilets hoping for an invitation.

On the toilet and elsewhere, Romans had little expectation of privacy. Space in cities was at a premium and public buildings occupied what today would be considered a disproportionate area of the city. The average urban home was not a *domus* but an *insula* – a large apartment block. Cooking fires were generally banned in the highly flammable apartment buildings, so a Roman city had an abundance of places to eat, from fast food to full-scale taverns where alcohol was served. With public facilities for bathing and other personal functions, a Roman's private space was generally needed only for sleeping and storing valuables and a change of clothes. Everyday Roman wear was a tunic, belted at the waist. In the absence of pockets, items were generally dropped down the neck of the tunic and retained by the belt. The toga was highly impractical and used only for formal occasions.

Many Roman pastimes can be partially reconstructed from archaeological remains. Children played with dolls, toy swords and even little cast lead gladiators. Adults enjoyed board games and above all, playing dice. The soldiers who threw dice for Christ's clothes at the crucifixion were playing a game enjoyed by all levels of society up to the emperor. As with the modern world, some games were private and others were huge spectacles played out before audiences numbering tens of thousands. The Romans had specific public buildings for public spectacles: arenas, theatres and circuses. The archetypal buildings in each case are to be found in Rome, from where the description is best drawn.

The theatre

> Don't let jeering critics attack him [the writer] from all sides but understand his situation. If you give him your undivided attention other playwrights will be encouraged to produce new works.
>
> Prologue (l.55-57) to Terence's comedy
> *The Mother-in-law*

Almost every Roman town of any size had a theatre. Rome's premier theatrical location was the Theatre of Marcellus. Built in Augustan times, this building has, through the ages, also acted as a weapons depot and a family fortress and today is a collection of apartments. Roman theatres generally faced north, as theatrical performances took place in the afternoon, and so patrons were protected from the summer sun by the high wall at their backs, while the sunlight illuminated the stage. Roman public displays might be advertised as *cum vela*, which meant that the seating area was screened from the sun. Aristocratic Romans liked smaller theatres, known as *odeons*, which featured singing, poetry recitations and traditional plays by writers such as Aeschylus or Sophocles, generally in the original Greek. The general public preferred bawdy slapstick pantomimes, often laden with political satire: one popular actor in Nero's time sang the popular song 'Goodbye mother, goodbye father' while miming eating and swimming; Nero was believed to have poisoned his father and tried to drown his mother.

The arena

> Aulus Suettius Certus has hired a gladiator troop which will
> fight on May 31. There will also be an animal hunt. The show
> is *cum vela*.
>
> Inscription from Pompeii (CIL 4.1190)

The building where gladiators fought had two parts: the oval
of sand ('sand' is *harena* in Latin) and the area where the spectators sat, which was the amphitheatre. *Amphi* means 'two', so the
oval arena was formed by two 'theatres' facing each other. Oval
was the optimal shape for an arena, as it allowed spectators a
remarkably intimate view of the action. Rome's premier arena
was within the Flavian amphitheatre, which Vespasian had built
on the remains of Nero's vainglorious palace. This entire area
was known as the Colosseum, after the gigantic statue that stood
beside the amphitheatre, but over the centuries the name was
transferred to the building itself.

Despite a popular modern misconception, gladiatorial shows
were not usually part of Roman public festivals; rather than being
regular bloodbaths, gladiatorial shows were relatively rare events.
Only the midwinter festival of the Saturnalia featured gladiators
as a standard feature. However, emperors were fond of tacking
'unofficial' games of their own on to official festivals and these
did feature gladiators. Nevertheless, most gladiators fought fewer
than half a dozen times a year.

The ethics of the arena have been a topic of recent debate.
To modern society the taking of life for entertainment is utterly
reprehensible but from the Roman perspective, none of the
blood shed in the arena was innocent; justice was being seen to be
done. Gladiators, for example, were dead men walking; men who
would otherwise have been executed for crimes such as banditry
or desertion from the army. For such men, the arena offered the
possibility of freedom by exceptional *virtus*, an indefinable quality

Figure 5   The Colosseum, Rome's bloodiest arena; memorably described by Charles Dickens as 'The ghost of old Rome, that wicked wonderful old city ... now a ruin, God be thanked, a ruin.' (Picture courtesy of Adrian Goldsworthy)

combining moral and physical strength, which the Romans prized highly. From a Roman perspective a gladiatorial fight was less about death than the struggle for redemption; fame and obscene wealth awaited a lucky few fighters. Most humans who died in the arena were *noxii*; condemned criminals. The Roman Empire had no police force and distinguished clearly between law, which was a matter for the individual, and order, which was enforced by militias, city guards and in extreme cases, by the legions. Consequently, for theft, or even murder, the aggrieved party had to bring the offender to court and oversee his prosecution. Because the state offered only limited protection against criminals, executions in the arena allowed the public to very publicly see justice done, and would-be malefactors to observe the possible consequences of their actions. Few were bothered that the condemned often died horribly; that was the point.

The Flavian Amphitheatre (the Colosseum) was a working arena for over two hundred years. More humans died in that one place than almost anywhere else on earth. Despite this, most of the blood shed was animal. Animal hunts were a part of Roman rural life and were re-enacted in the arena for the benefit of townsfolk. The more dangerous and exotic the creatures killed, the more the crowd enjoyed the spectacle. Even in the late Republic, Cicero commented that Asia Minor was being depopulated of panthers to feed the arenas of the empire. However, he did not feel this was a great loss; in the countryside of the Roman Empire, bears and wolves were common and Romans felt more in need of protection from these species than an urge to protect them.

The circuses – arenas for chariot racing

> The racetrack, with its top-notch horses, there in the densely packed circus.
>
> Ovid, *Art of Love* 1.135–136

The Flavian Amphitheatre could comfortably seat about fifty thousand people, though it has been speculated that up to eighty thousand might have squeezed in on occasion. However, the arena was not the main passion of the Roman people: that was chariot racing. Rome's biggest chariot-racing venue was the Circus Maximus, where as many as 150,000 spectators might watch a race, but there were also at least two other lesser venues. The imperial quarters on the Palatine overlooked the racetrack, making it possible for the emperor to watch the races from the comfort of his palace. Poor families sometimes picnicked on the lower slopes of the hill where they enjoyed an inferior, but also free, view.

Chariot racers worked in teams, known by their identifying colours: the Blues, the Greens, the Reds and the Whites. Other team colours were occasionally added but only these four proved durable enough to last the entire history of the Roman Empire and well into the Byzantine era. Supporters were vociferous and riots between groups with different affiliations were not uncommon. The races have been depicted in numerous bas reliefs, mosaics and poetry, giving a reasonably clear picture of how events unfolded. The most popular races were between four-horse chariots, which were little more than platforms of hardened leather on wheels. The charioteer wore light leather armour and steered his horses with the reins wrapped around his waist. Many charioteers were slaves, though like gladiators, a popular charioteer could rise to the heights of popular acclaim, as this obituary shows:

> I am Scorpus, the glory of the roaring Circus, the much-applauded but short-lived darling of Rome. Jealous Fate counted my victories instead of my years and carried me off aged twenty-six.

Martial, Epigrams 10.53

As with gladiators, charioteers stood a very high chance of death or serious injury. Collisions were frequent and dramatic and the light armour afforded little protection. Such a disaster almost certainly claimed the life of Scorpus.

Between races the audience were sometimes entertained by clowns, trick riders, animal displays or executions, which – apart from the last – are also features of the modern circus. St Peter was executed at the Circus of Nero, which the emperor had built on the Vatican hill to privately indulge his passion for driving chariots. The martyr was buried in the graveyard directly outside the Circus, where his tomb became a pilgrim destination almost immediately. One of the obelisks from Nero's racetrack stands today outside the Vatican church that was later raised over St Peter's grave.

4

The time of crises

Near at hand
Is the end of the world and the last day
And judgement of immortal God for such
as are both called and chosen. First of all
Inexorable wrath shall fall on Rome
A time of blood and wretched life shall come
Woe, woe to thee, O land of Italy
Great, barbarous nation.

> Sibylline Oracles 8.91–95

> M.S. Terry (NY 1890) quoted in Lewis &
> Reinhold, *Roman Civilization* 1966, p. 416

What is generally referred to as the third-century crisis was a time of great instability – sometimes bordering on anarchy – which gripped the Roman Empire between the death of Caracalla in 217 and the accession of Diocletian in 284. Signs that all was not well were evident during the reign of Marcus Aurelius (161–180 CE) and became yet more apparent during the disastrous reign of Marcus Aurelius' son Commodus. However, the mini-crisis which followed the assassination of Commodus was followed by the stable and highly successful rule of Rome's most underrated emperor, Septimius Severus (193–211 CE), whose steady hand temporarily masked Rome's increasing problems.

The crisis was actually at least three separate crises, which partly overlapped and exacerbated each other. Casting the third century as a period of unrelieved anarchy and unrest ignores the fact that many of the fundamental strengths of the empire remained. Stereotyping change as decline hinders understanding of major social changes in this period; changes still felt today in modern Europe.

The end of an era

The first crisis was political. Signs of this were evident before 180 CE; for example when Avidius Cassius declared himself emperor in the east in 175, after a false report that Marcus Aurelius was dead. Political crises were no new phenomenon; arguably they had been a feature of the Roman Empire since its inception. The issue lay dormant during the long era of imperial peace but revived in its most deadly form with the death of Marcus Aurelius and continued for as long as the western empire. The second crisis was military. Some historians claim that the *pax Romana*, the Roman peace, ended in 180 CE with the death of Marcus Aurelius. Certainly this was the opinion of the great English historian Edward Gibbon. However, there were large-scale conflicts with both western barbarians and organised Parthian armies before 180 CE. Thereafter, these conflicts grew in strength and frequency and never completely ceased until the western empire itself had ended. The third crisis was economic: the army cost more than the Roman Empire could afford and its costs rose even as the army became less competent at keeping the peace and the war-ravaged provinces of the empire became less able to shoulder the financial strain.

Each crisis fed off the others, yet each had a separate beginning and end. The solutions were not the same for each but a single factor which underlay all three was the fatal failure of the Roman Empire: the flawed imperial succession process.

The political crisis

> After his [Aurelian's] death, the legions sent messages to the senate asking them to select an emperor ... The senate replied that this was a right which belonged to the legions themselves.
>
> Flavius Vopsicus, *Life of Aurelian* 40.2–3

The Roman imperial system was an elaborate façade that made the real issues hard for contemporaries to identify, let alone resolve. Improvisation by Augustus had resulted in the creation of the principate; an autocracy that looked like a republic.

The republican façade became increasingly flimsy as the first century went on, yet its existence prevented discussion of the question of how a *princeps,* who technically was a private citizen, could designate a successor. On what criteria could a successor be chosen, when properly speaking he had no office to succeed to? Trial and error eventually produced a rough consensus that an emperor's son could attempt to rule on his father's death. Lacking a son, the emperor should adopt one in good time for the imperial heir to be recognised. The façade endured through the second century, concealing the brutal reality that from Julius Caesar onwards, Rome was a military dictatorship. Julius Caesar and Augustus gained power not through constitutional process but by armed force. The apocryphal story that Septimius Severus told his sons to 'stand by each other, take care of the army and let the rest go hang' shows people had few illusions about the nature of imperial rule.

Later, selection by the army became the de facto form of succession. When an emperor perished – and in the third century most lasted just a few years – parts of the army would each declare their candidate as successor. Sometimes the rival claims were resolved without bloodshed (apart from that of the unsuccessful candidate) and sometimes the issue was settled by a brisk civil war. Generally, once that was sorted out, the senate would promote the successful candidate from 'pretender' to 'emperor'. In short, by the third century the constitutional façade had crumbled. As a historical convenience, rather than an actual clear dividing-line, the end of the Augustan-style principate is generally considered to be 235 CE, when the last Severan emperor was killed and replaced by Maximinus. No one pretended that Maximinus became *princeps* in recognition of his exceptional qualities or that he guided the state by force of character. Like almost every third-century emperor, Maximinus was kept in power by his troops. Third-century emperors spent most of their careers on campaign and were frequently killed in the process, usually by their own men. Nevertheless, there was never a shortage of nominees to replace both dead and current emperors and the constant civil wars that resulted enfeebled the army and distracted it from coping with external threats.

Political instability and military anarchy

But on his arrival he found that the legions were ready to mutiny and accordingly he ordered them to be disbanded ... thereupon some soldiers murdered him ... many give different accounts but it is generally agreed that those who killed him were soldiers, for they hurled many insults at him, speaking of him as a child and of his mother as greedy and covetous.

Aelius Lampridus,
Life of Severus Alexander 59 (excerpts)

The term 'military anarchy' was coined in 1926 by the Russian historian Rostovtzeff to describe the period between the death of Alexander Severus, (the last of the Severans, killed by his troops in 235 CE) and the beginning of the rule of Diocletian in 284 CE. This period was marked by three major characteristics – the decline of the senate, the fragmentation of the empire and massive barbarian incursions.

As ever, the military and economic crises complicated and exacerbated the political crisis. The army had become more parochial, partly because Septimius Severus had broken with precedent and allowed serving soldiers to marry and have families. This gave soldiers a vested interest in the communities where they were based and a strong disinclination to leave their families undefended, no matter how urgently they were needed elsewhere. Second, the financial crisis made soldiers more dependent on local sources of supplies, which were levied as taxation in kind. This also tied the legions to a particular locality and gave them an incentive to defend it. The troops of a particular region hoped that a general promoted to emperor by their efforts would favour them and their region. In reality, a region generally suffered for supporting a pretender to imperial power. If successful, the pretender took the army away to support his claims to the rest of the empire. If not, troops supporting a rival treated the region as enemy territory. In either case, the invasion of imperial troops or opportunistic barbarians meant economic devastation and the inevitable human suffering and loss of life.

There was a further cost to the political crisis, which historians have only recently noted: that to the empire's upper classes. Whenever rebellion broke out, influential people close to a pretender had to choose their allegiance. A wrong choice led to the confiscation of property (all emperors of the period desperately needed money and were happy to confiscate it from the supporters of their rivals) and at worse to the execution of the entire family. Even the right choice was hazardous: it identified a person with the current ruler, so he became suspect when that ruler was violently deposed. The upper classes of Rome had always run this risk, but in the third century the frequent turnover of emperors caused massive attrition of the aristocracy. This attrition affected the vibrant civic life that had been a feature of earlier eras. Fewer people were prepared to accept positions of authority that identified them with the current regime. There was also a financial disincentive: those in authority were charged with collecting the ever-increasing taxes needed to support the army, and local dignitaries often had to make good shortfalls in tax revenue from their own pockets.

Taxes were rising because an empire at war with itself and wracked by barbarian invasions became less productive. Consequently, those still able to pay taxes had to pay more. Those paying the high taxes felt that they were entitled to protection by the soldiers they were paying for, and they passed these sentiments on to local units of the army. In 258 CE the 'fight local' sentiment reached its logical conclusion. A general, Postumus, was in charge of the Rhine frontier while the emperor Gallienus dealt with revolts along the Danube. Probably fearing that they would be required to leave the Rhine undefended should the emperor summon them (there was also a crisis with Persia), soldiers of the Gallic army declared Postumus emperor. No emperor of the period would tolerate a pretender, no matter how unwilling, so Postumus became 'emperor' whether he wanted to or not.

Neither Postumus nor his army were interested in conquering the rest of the empire. Their focus was on Gaul, Britain and Spain, which the army protected from invasion, whether by barbarians or the indignant Gallienus (the emperor's son had died in the course of his coup). Gallienus gave up trying to reclaim the lost territory after a single failed attempt, mainly because he was fully occupied with barbarian invasions in Germania, Pannonia and Dacia. The eastern section of the empire also took advantage of the current crisis to become semi-autonomous under the leadership of Odenathus of Palmyra. The Roman Empire briefly became three separate political entities, each with its own ruler and bureaucratic institutions. Though the empire was later reunited, this break-up foreshadowed the more formal division of the empire in the fourth century.

Political fragmentation, social unity

I grant Roman citizenship throughout the world ... so that no one should remain outside the citizen body ... for it is proper that the masses should help share the burden and share also in the victory.

Extract from Caracalla's 'universal citizenship' decree.
Giessen Papyrus 40 col 1

The Roman Empire might have permanently broken apart in 260 CE but there were two main reasons why it did not. The first was that after Gallienus, a succession of 'soldier emperors' from Dalmatia and Pannonia halted the slide towards anarchy. Aurelian (270–275 CE) came to power by deposing the hapless successor of his commander Claudius Gothicus (who had died of the plague) and defeating the invading tribes that crossed the Rhine and Danube frontiers.

In 272, with the barbarians temporarily beaten into quiescence, Aurelian turned on the breakaway faction on Rome's eastern frontier. Odenathus had been assassinated and Queen Zenobia of Palmyra was acting as regent for her son, Vaballathus. Zenobia's defiance of the imperial regime was becoming increasingly blatant. Although nominally a Roman subject, she sent her troops to take command of Egypt and Asia Minor. When Aurelian's hostility became clear, Zenobia became an outright rebel, but it quickly became apparent that Palmyran political aspirations were no match for Aurelian's military might.

With Palmyra subdued, Aurelian marched west against the 'Gallic Empire'. He defeated Tetricus, a successor to Postumus (who had been murdered by his soldiers for refusing to allow them to sack a rebel Gallic city). Sources for the period refer to Aurelian's legendary cruelty, but this may be a later Christian tradition, for Aurelian was planning to persecute Christians when he was assassinated. Certainly, his treatment of Tetricus and Zenobia was mild; both were spared and Tetricus was even given a minor administrative post in Italy. Aurelian was eventually killed by his officers, but under his successors the military situation continued to improve. Seven years and six emperors after Aurelian's assassination, Diocletian came to power and completed the political stabilisation of the empire, ruling for nearly two decades before becoming the only emperor in history to retire voluntarily.

Although short-lived, Rome's emperors were militarily competent, which is one reason the empire survived civil wars and repeated barbarian invasions. The other reason was that, by and large, those within the empire considered themselves Roman and had no inclination to separate themselves from their fellow citizens. Even the breakaway empire of the Gauls was a temporary response to a military emergency. Once Aurelian made it plain that he was willing and able to take care of the western portions of the empire, the people there accepted his rule with little complaint (though Tetricus' army put up a stiff fight).

In part the unity of the empire was due to Caracalla, son of Septimius Severus. In 212 CE, the Edict of Caracalla extended Roman citizenship to all free men and women under his rule; the culmination of the spread of Roman citizenship in previous centuries. By Caracalla's day, Roman citizenship indicated membership of a shared culture rather than affiliation to the city of Rome. Caracalla's intent was not the altruistic ideal of making all within the empire members of one vast Roman family, although to some extent that is what happened. His aims were more pragmatic. First, only Roman citizens could serve in the legions, so at a stroke the Edict enlarged the pool of potential military manpower. Second, even as he increased the number of Roman citizens, Caracalla doubled the inheritance tax, the army's main source of revenue.

However pragmatic the motivation, the Edict recognised an underlying reality: the Roman Empire was now more united by a common culture than divided by regional differences. A knowledge of Latin and Greek served travellers from the Thames to the Euphrates and coins minted in Britain could be exchanged in Alexandria. The deeds of contemporary folk heroes, such as Apollodorus of Tydna, circulated through the entire empire, as did the writings of playwrights, poets and historians. The Edict also brought all the free peoples of the empire under the single edifice of Roman law, creating a legal system that not only survived the break-up of the empire but became the foundation of the legal systems of modern Europe. Greeks, Gauls and Libyans were now Romans, not merely living under the rule of Rome. Even the short-lived breakaway regimes of the third century set themselves up as Roman-style states. In Gaul, the emperor appointed consuls and had his own version of the senate, although the situation in Palmyra is less certain. If, in the third century, genuine nationalist and separatist sentiments had been widespread, Rome's empire would certainly have fragmented beyond recovery.

Emperors and senators

The senate was so afraid of him [Maximinus Thrax (235–238), the first emperor never to set foot in Rome] that prayers were made in the temples both publicly and privately and even by women together with their children, that he should never see the city of Rome.

Julius Capitolinus, *Life of the Maximini* 8.6

Another aspect of the political crisis of the third century was the changing role of the emperor. Emperors became primarily army commanders. When almost every military success led to the commander being declared emperor by the victorious troops, the emperor's only chance of survival was to assume the role of the victorious commander whom the troops praised.

In the first and second centuries the emperors (apart from the peripatetic Hadrian) had made only rare excursions to the provinces. In the third century, emperors were rarely in Rome, because the army was desperately needed elsewhere and it was essential for his personal well-being that the emperor commanded the army. This reduced the political role of the senate which stayed in Rome while the emperor was in the field and communication between the two pillars of government was often delayed and difficult. The third-century historian Herodian summed things up: 'Rome is where the emperor is.' The senate is believed to have originally been the *concilium* – the advisory council – of the archaic kings of Rome. By the third century, the senate was largely obsolete; the *concilium* of the emperor in the field had more practical power. Cities and provincial governors in need of guidance or assistance sent envoys directly to the emperor, wherever he might be; the senate was – usually – informed retrospectively of the imperial decision. More and more, the senate became simply the city council of Rome, albeit a council with huge prestige and some highly influential members.

Senators also lost control of the army to professional commanders. There were several reasons for this. First, in a crisis the emperor could not waste a talented general simply because he was not a senator. Second, until the third century those made emperor were invariably senators, so ruling emperors took the obvious step of ensuring that few senators were given armies to lead against them. (This stratagem failed: the army simply started choosing non-senatorial emperors starting with Macrinus, who took power in 217 when Caracalla was assassinated.) Finally, the most essential quality in a third-century army commander was loyalty to the emperor. The emperor tended to trust those he knew personally. The senate was in Rome and the emperor generally wasn't, so it followed that the emperor trusted few senators. In fact, according to some reports the emperor Gallienus actually barred senators from military service.

Formerly, the commander of a legion, the *legatus*, was a senator or at least of a senatorial family, but this position now went to a professional full-time military officer. Likewise, whereas provincial governors had once automatically commanded the legions within their provinces, there was a tendency to separate military and imperial commands, a trend which became official policy under Diocletian, by which time few provincial governors were senators. While the senate as a body steadily lost power during the third century, individual senators did not. In times of crisis the rich tend to get richer and the poor get poorer. In the Roman Empire senators used their influence – diminished but still great – to obtain relief from taxation. They generally used slave labour to farm their very extensive estates and so these estates flourished even as free farmers were conscripted into the army. Wealthy senators purchased farms and smallholdings devastated by barbarians or hostile imperial troops and rebuilt them. Other senators simply took by force lands where the previous owners were too powerless or too dead to complain.

The military crisis

The cities of Italy had long ago exchanged walls for the enduring peace of Roman citizenship. But now they were forced by necessity to restore the walls from their ruined state and raise towers and ramparts.

Herodian *Roman History* 8.2.4

The exact size of the Roman army during the third century is uncertain, though it was tiny, relative to the population and the length of the frontiers it defended. At the height of the third-century crisis, it probably numbered between three and four hundred thousand men. They guarded a frontier that stretched over four thousand kilometres, from the River Tyne to the Tigris and defended a population of some fifty million civilians. As a very rough comparison, Britain at the end of the Second World War, in 1945, had a comparable population but three million men under arms, almost ten times the Roman figure.

There were good reasons why the Roman army was not larger. First, for almost a millennium the Roman state had grown and prospered with an army of this size or smaller. The Rome of earlier eras had fought few defensive wars and even they consisted of aggressively seeking out and confronting an invading army. In these circumstances, the concentration and effective use of force was more important than the overall size of the army. Every Roman schoolchild learned how in 69 BCE Licinius Lucullus had routed an Armenian army of up to a quarter of a million men using just twenty-five thousand highly motivated legionaries and some auxiliary cavalry.

The second reason is logistic. The industrialised nations of the twentieth century were capable of supporting large armies in the field but Rome had neither the infrastructure nor technology. Even a legion of three to six thousand men (Roman legions were rarely full strength) considerably distorted the regional economy that supported it. Sitting quietly in its barracks, a legion consumed around twelve tonnes of grain a day; an army in the field also needed fresh water and resupplies of kit and equipment. Even if Rome could raise millions of men, it could not get them where they needed to be before they died of thirst and starvation.

Third, even if logistical problems could be overcome, financial constraints made a larger army impossible because Rome could not properly pay even for the army it had. One of the first requirements for a standing army is that the society supporting it has a food surplus to feed it. Yet in antiquity, entire populations could face famine after a poor harvest. A society with a standing army also needs an economic surplus with which to pay and equip the men. Since every item used by the Roman army was hand-made by individual artisans, the cost of supplying and maintaining weapons, armour, clothing and housing was much higher per soldier than in a modern industrialised civilisation. The unstable political situation meant that soldiers could and did demand high wages and regular bonuses from the emperors whom they kept in power. The cost of the army absorbed almost all the income of the imperial coffers. Even a modest addition of forty thousand men might bankrupt the state. In the third century this presented a dilemma: Rome could hardly afford the soldiers it had and yet it needed more, even though these soldiers were a major reason for the crisis.

The enemies of Rome

The Gepids, Greuthungrians and Vandals; all broke their treaties. For when [the emperor] Probus was preoccupied with wars with usurpers they rampaged across the entire world on foot or in ships and more than somewhat dented the glory of Rome.

Flavius Vopsicus, *Life of Probus* 18.2

The biggest threat to the Roman Empire of the third century was Rome itself. The civil wars of the dysfunctional political system regularly purged the army of capable officers who had ended up on the wrong side, and pitted legionary against legionary when both were desperately needed on the frontier. When the legions were distracted, outsiders sensed an opportunity. The

Whom are you calling 'a barbarian'?

The Romans of the imperial era used 'barbarian' to mean 'other than of Graeco-Roman culture' and the term encompassed cultures such as Sassanian and Chinese which were in some ways more advanced and civilised than the Romans themselves.

'Barbarian' is a generally non-pejorative term used to describe particular tribal groups and cultures, especially those living north and east of the Rhine and Danube frontiers. These barbarians were often not particularly 'barbaric' – one of the greatest generals of late Rome, Stilicho, had a Vandal father; many others were Christians who understood Latin.

chaos of the mid-third century caused the barbarian peoples at the empire's edge to see Rome not as a threat to be feared but as a target to be plundered.

There is considerable debate as to the size and nature of the 'barbarian menace'. On the Rhine and Danube the Goths were a continual threat. In earlier years, this tribe had (according to its legends) been a relatively undistinguished grouping, living somewhere in Scandinavia. During the first century, they moved south-eastward and grew in strength. The first archaeological evidence shows that early second century Goths moved westward along the Vistula towards the Roman frontier, displacing other tribes. This disruption of German tribal arrangements may have caused Rome's problems with the Quadi and Marcomani, which took Marcus Aurelius to Germania at the end of the second century in a failed attempt to restore peace to a region which had been semi-quiescent for almost a century.

In the mid-third century the Goths reached, and repeatedly breached, the Roman frontier, especially in Asia Minor and the Balkans. Theirs was not an organised assault under a single leader, for the Goths formed a loose confederation, as inclined to fight each other as the Romans. Nevertheless, they were the first of the large tribal groupings that plagued the empire until its fall. The

Goths who arrived on the Black Sea coast rapidly formed huge fleets, which came close to wiping out the Roman settlements there. Eventually, this fleet broke through the Hellespont to raid the length of the littoral of Asia Minor. The Goths' success in raiding deep within Roman territory encouraged other tribes, such as the Carpi or Sarmatian Iazyges, to follow suit. Rome's military response was handicapped by its dysfunctional politics. This is epitomised by an occasion in 248, when a mixture of Goths, Carpi and lesser Germanic tribes took advantage of a minor provincial revolt to flood into the Danube provinces. The emperor, Philip the Arab (244–249), sent a powerful army, led by Gaius Decius, a distinguished Roman senator, to restore order. It was increasingly rare for senators to command armies and Decius' men showed why, by promptly declaring him emperor. This forced Decius into a military confrontation with Philip the Arab at a time when every legionary was desperately needed at the Danube.

Decius' and Philip the Arab's armies met near Verona in 249 and Philip was killed. By the time Decius marched against the barbarians, they had completed their pillage of the virtually defenceless Danube provinces and withdrawn over the frontier. They came back two years later under King Cniva – the first Gothic leader whose name is securely established – and plundered their way to Thrace, where the Roman army predictably rebelled and set up its governor as emperor. After initial successes, Decius and his son fell in action against the Goths at the battle of Abrittus (in modern Bulgaria). This succession of events demonstrates that large-scale barbarian invasions were a problem because Rome failed to respond coherently. There is an edifying comparison with the late Roman Republic, when in the late second century BCE Rome faced a massive Cimbric invasion. Despite losing several battles and well over 100,000 men, the Republic retained its political will, raised further armies and eventually turned the tide, virtually exterminating the Cimbri in a series of battles in northern Italy.

There is no reason to believe that the Goths were more numerous than the Cimbri, which the Romans of the Republic threw back with fewer resources. Many academics no longer regard barbarian pressure as the primary cause of Rome's difficulties in the third century, or the western empire's collapse in the fifth. When politically healthy, the Roman Republic and early empire had coped with equivalent threats but three hundred and fifty years after the Cimbric invasions, no Roman emperor could trust any army he did not lead personally (and not always then). Confronted with more than one threat, no sane emperor would divide his army to confront each threat separately. Therefore, emperors concentrated the army under their command, dealing with one usurper or barbarian incursion at a time and sometimes bribing other invaders to withdraw. The price of a failing body politic was paid in looted provinces and a devastated economy.

It did not take Rome's enemies long to realise that Rome could cope with just one military problem at a time. An attack or rebellion anywhere in the empire became the signal for others to take advantage. Rome's inability to deal with more than one military emergency in fact usually guaranteed that several emergencies happened at once. Barbarian incursions penetrated the empire deeply enough for not only Italy but even Rome to come under threat, as the emperor Aurelian recognised in 271, when he constructed the first new defensive walls around the city for almost a millennium. Walls were an effective defence against barbarian invaders, as Germans and Goths had little ability at siege craft. However, while walls ensured a relative degree of safety for the cities of the west, the same was not true on Rome's eastern frontier. There, the enemy was neither disorganised nor uncivilised and was very good at sieges.

The repeated Roman invasions of the Parthian Empire in the first and second centuries had caused political and military disruption, especially the invasions of Trajan, Marcus Aurelius' co-emperor Lucius Verus, and Septimius Severus (who is commemorated in the Arch of Severus, which today stands by the senate house in the Roman Forum) and his son Caracalla. The invasions of Lucius Verus and Septimius Severus were contemporary with a devastating plague in Parthia, possibly the first appearance of smallpox in the west. The Roman army imported this plague into the empire, where it killed five thousand people a day in Rome alone. The plague contributed to the subsequent weakness of the Roman Empire and killed at least one emperor: Claudius Gothicus, who died in 270. The effect on the Parthian Empire is unrecorded but presumably was equally debilitating.

The last great Roman invasion of Parthia collapsed with the emperor Caracalla's assassination in 217. However, the increasing feebleness of Parthian rule led to a resurgence of the Persian people in the area of modern Iran. Ardashir I, the Persian leader, defeated the Parthian king in battle and subsumed the Parthian Empire under the rule of his own people. These people styled themselves the successors of the Achaemenid Persian Empire (overthrown by Alexander the Great in the 330s BCE), although the culture of the empire remained closer to the Parthians. The name given to these Persians today is 'Sassanian' or 'Sassanid', after Sasan, the first of the family of Iranian kings to rebel against the Parthians. It is often assumed that the Sassanians were a dynamic and militarily organised people whose efficiency in battle starkly contrasted with the generally chaotic Parthian military. However, at its peak the Parthians generally held their own against Rome, while some of the greatest Sassanian successes came during the third century, when Rome made Parthia look like a model state. It did not help the third-century Romans that Ardashir's son was the capable and long-lived Shapur I, whose rule of thirty years spanned the middle of the century and the reigns of over a dozen Roman emperors and pretenders.

These emperors included the wretched Valerian (253–260), taken prisoner by Shapur after the battle of Edessa, and becoming the only Roman emperor to die in foreign captivity. Valerian had been forced to attack Shapur because the Sassanians claimed the full territory of the old Achaemenid Empire, parts of which had been held by the Seleucids and Romans for five hundred years or more. Shapur attacked Syria and plundered Antioch, one of the greatest cities of the east, and was kept from further successes not by an organised response by the Roman central government but by the ad hoc defence of the capable Odenathus of Palmyra. Shapur's death coincided with the beginnings of Rome's gradual recovery. Thereafter, failed Sassanian military adventures against the Illyrian soldier-emperors who spearheaded Rome's recovery reversed most of the gains made under Shapur. Nevertheless, the Sassanian Persians remained a threat to the Roman Empire's eastern frontier well into the Byzantine era, when they were replaced by the first Islamic caliphate.

Although the Sassanians were firmly categorised as 'barbarian' by the Romans, their civilisation contained both original thinkers and repositories of ancient culture. These repositories included Greek philosophical texts lost to the west, which were only redis-covered in the late Middle Ages. Sassanian art and textiles were of superb quality and a trade-based economic system backed the Sassanian armies with financial muscle.

Dura-Europos

The effectiveness of the Sassanian Persians at siege warfare is vividly illustrated by the remains of the fortress city of Dura-Europos on the Euphrates River, in modern Syria. This citadel was attacked and destroyed by Shapur in 256 and then abandoned, so the Persian trenches and galleries, mines and siege ramp have been preserved for modern archaeologists to discover. In 2009, researchers at the University of Leicester found evidence that Persian scientists had concocted a sulphur-based poison gas that killed the Romans working on a counter-mine.

The economic crisis

> Nobody in the world should have any money but I, so that I
> can give it to the soldiers ... we no longer have any sources of
> revenue, legitimate or illegal but as long as we have this [the
> sword] we won't want for money.
>
> Caracalla in Cassius Dio 76.10

The Roman Empire rarely balanced its budget. This was in stark
contrast to the Roman Republic, which was so profitable that
Italy was largely free of taxes. However, the Roman Republic did
not generate profits through superior economic strength but by
seizing others' wealth. The later years of the Roman Republic
saw not just the expansion of the Roman Empire into Egypt,
Greece and Asia Minor but also a massive transfer of wealth and
slaves from these captured provinces to Rome. For some modern
scholars it is no coincidence that the borders of the empire
closely matched the limits beyond which expansion became
unprofitable. The frontiers of the empire were economic boundaries. When it ran out of wealthy Mediterranean civilisations to
loot, the Roman economy ran at a loss. This problem was partly
resolved by keeping down the size of the army and partly by
gently inflating the currency by diluting the amount of silver in
a standard *denarius*.

The third century greatly exacerbated the financial problems
of the Roman Empire but it did not cause them. Like the succession issue, the financial structure was flawed from the outset but
the strains of the third century made the flaws obvious. Even as
it became less effective at fending off foreign invaders, the army
became vastly more expensive. One reason for the rapid turnover
of emperors was that the army had a perverse incentive to continue
the process. Any candidate for emperor who wanted to survive
even nomination had to buy the loyalty of his troops with what is
known as a 'succession donative', a large cash payment, estimated

to be more than a year's wages for each legionary. A rebel governor would first empty the provincial treasury for the donative and then hope that whatever rival he defeated had enough left in his war chest for a further donative to buy the loyalty of his beaten army. Some soldiers were paid a donative every time their candidate was defeated, when they changed sides, or when they killed off their current leader. It was not a process that encouraged stability.

Furthermore, Septimius Severus had raised the salary of his soldiers – the first pay rise in a century – and Caracalla raised it again. Thus, the basic operating expenses of the army increased just as the imperial economy was collapsing. And not only the army but also administration became more expensive. Third-century Roman governments were very insecure, so bureaucratic jobs multiplied steadily. Offering plum government jobs to potential supporters is a technique for holding power which has become no less popular over the millennia. Another tendency of insecure governments is to heavily manage the lives of those they govern; this was as apparent in the third century as it is today. Splitting military command from the civil role of the provincial governor both created a further layer of administration to be filled with aspiring candidates and allowed imperial subjects to be supervised more closely. The cost to the public was two-fold. Bribery, and what would today be considered corruption, were recognised ways of interacting with authority and the expanded officialdom meant that citizens had more officials to bribe even as they supported the enlarged bureaucracy through their taxes:

> Administrators, secretaries, supervisors ... all these titles are taken by those who bring no financial advantage to the state but fatten themselves on the public purse.
>
> *Oxyrhynchus Papyrus* LCL 58, 288 CE

Emperors could not balance the budget, yet for most of the third century taxation did not greatly increase, because the greater part of the population already lived on a financial knife edge. Therefore, higher taxes invited large-scale civil dissent. It was probably zealous tax collectors who sparked the rebellions in Africa that brought the emperors Gordian I and Gordian II to power. To remain in power, a new emperor needed the support of financially-secure members of the upper class, so little of the very wealthy's cash could be siphoned off by the taxman. The minority who possessed a modicum of wealth without the concomitant political connections (such as, notoriously, the officials on many town and city councils) were swiftly taxed out of existence.

Even cutting back public spending was difficult. A common theme on the coinage of new or prospective emperors (apart from desperate and generally false assertions about the loyalty of the army) is *fortuna redux* 'the return of the good times'. Emperors were expected to be generous, indeed lavish in their expenditure, even in the face of grim financial reality. Despite the better times of the first century CE, the Emperor Galba's ham-fisted attempt at austerity in 69 CE not only failed to re-establish the imperial finances but also led directly to revolution and a fresh bout of expensive political and military convulsions.

Those attempting to rule in the third century had the additional disadvantage that they lacked the resources available in better times. Entire provinces were sometimes ruled by usurpers or rivals, or overrun and devastated by barbarian invaders. One successful revenue-raising technique practised from the bloody birth of the imperial era was proscription, a brutal system in which a new regime made a list of its enemies and then killed them. The killing was followed by the confiscation of the property of the newly deceased. A coup, successful or otherwise, usually meant that wealthy members of Roman society on the losing side would be stripped of their property and, incidentally, of their lives. In the long term, this had the unhealthy effect of concentrating wealth in the hands of a small bloc of those powerful enough to resist imperial predation; but in the third century few emperors had the luxury of considering the long term.

Two other ways existed to mitigate the cost of the army. One was pillage, when an army on the move took whatever it needed from the province through which it was passing, whether the province was friendly or hostile. When the army stopped for any length of time, the soldiers were billeted in whatever town had paid least to avoid the imposition. From the point of view of damage to the local economy, it mattered little whether the army moving through a region was defending or invading it. Alternatively, poverty-stricken emperors could debase the currency, as administrations in financial distress have done over the millennia (and do today). Under the Republic the basic coin of the empire – the *denarius* – was nearly pure silver. The profligate Nero produced beautiful coins, which compensated in artistic merit for being debased by almost five percent. In the time of Trajan a silver *denarius* deserved ninety percent of that description, but by the time of Marcus Aurelius the silver content had dipped below seventy-five percent. Septimius Severus paid for the higher salaries of his soldiers by dropping the silver content of coins to fifty percent and Caracalla had the clever idea of introducing the two-*denarius* coin, which had only one-and-a-half times the silver content of a single *denarius*. As financial pressures on the empire increased, the value of the denarius went into freefall. By the time matters stabilised somewhat under the soldier-emperor Aurelian, some coins had a silver content close to one percent. The decreasing worth of the *denarius* had another effect on soldiers permanently located in a particular area. Since it was impractical to destroy the means of production of the people who were feeding them, soldiers took to imposing taxation in kind, with crops and other materials paid directly to the army without reference to the central authorities.

How much this financial crisis mattered is now hard to tell. Records from the third century are patchy and unreliable, where they exist at all. Logic assumes that rampant inflation must have devastated the economic life of the empire, but this is the logic of the twenty-first century. In the ancient world, some communities may simply have reverted to pre-imperial financial systems or successfully built rising prices into their financial lives. Symptoms of apparent economic decline can be explained in other ways. The number of inscriptions in urban areas is lower in quantity and quality but inscriptions may have gone out of fashion. An inscription would be an indelible record of the political affiliation of the person who commissioned it and such commitment was dangerous in times of political flux. The number of known third-century shipwrecks is markedly lower than in the first century. This might suggest reduced long-distance trade but might also reflect the archaeological sites explored or even improved ship-building techniques by the ancients. Furthermore, goods such as fine pottery were widely manufactured in the provinces, making imports unnecessary. Evidence for the abandonment of some rural communities and the shrinking of urban centres might reflect changing settlement patterns or the effects of plague, rather than economic damage. The lack of third-century Roman coin finds in India might tell us that trade with the orient dropped precipitously or it might tell us that orientals preferred payment in plain gold to debased Roman specie. Despite the possible explanations for each individual symptom of decline, historians of the third century are not required to explain evidence for growth and prosperity because almost no evidence exists. Therefore, it is an acceptable conclusion that the main reason for evidence of economic failure in the third century is that the third-century economy was failing.

A century of change

The unrelieved litany of woe which we find in our sources for the third century contrasts dramatically with the peace and prosperity of the preceding century. However, the claim that the collapse of Rome was only averted by the powerful personalities of 'soldier emperors' such as Aurelian, Carus and Diocletian can be challenged on a number of counts.

First, even as state institutions buckled under various crises, the people of the Roman Empire firmly believed in Rome as a collective social enterprise worth maintaining. Second, we must consider what has been termed 'the rhetoric of decline'. It was a truism of ancient society that the world was running down. No Roman considered himself the man his ancestors had been and the world itself was a worn-out relic of a long-gone golden age, collapsing into ruin. Those who perpetrated Rome's literary tradition in the third century largely belonged to a senatorial class with a vastly diminished role in state affairs. For them, the current state of affairs was both a reflection and consequence of the reduced role of the senate and their polemic strongly accentuated the negative.

The third century undoubtedly experienced a number of crises, generally the consequence of unresolved flaws in the imperial system. However, detailed work by archaeologists over the past century has revealed a number of bright spots in the gloom and shown that the Roman Empire retained many of its fundamental strengths.

For example, changing settlement and agricultural patterns in Spain may reflect not imperial decline but the dramatic success of the rival province of Africa. Africa became a major economic force in the third century and took over many functions which Spain had once performed in the imperial economic system. Untouched by warfare and with crop production brought to new heights of productivity by sophisticated agricultural techniques and irrigation, Africa flourished and exported much of its economic surplus to Rome.

Another success story of empire was Britain, where improved deep-ploughing techniques allowed high yields of grain from formerly relatively unproductive heavy loam and clay. This may explain why, despite increasing prosperity, urbanism in Britain declined as elite members of society moved from the cities to the villa estates which had become the foundation of the British economy. It is also not coincidental that at this time Britain, like Africa, was relatively unplagued by warfare and its concomitant damage to infrastructure and therefore enjoyed a competitive economic advantage. Finally, even if the Roman Empire as a whole had declined from the golden age of the second century, the decline was relative. Rome remained sophisticated and highly productive, economically, numerically and militarily not only superior to its immediate neighbours but also to any state in Europe for the next thousand years.

However, things were not seen this way at the time, because the conservative Romans felt that change was invariably for the worse and this period certainly saw wrenching change. Their point of view was exacerbated by the new religious beliefs sweeping the empire. Christianity – the most influential of these religions – firmly endorsed the belief that people were living in the 'end times', with an apocalypse and final reckoning close at hand.

Religious and cultural developments

Be ashamed, Roman people everywhere, be ashamed of the lives that you lead! ... The barbarians do not conquer us with the strength of their bodies, nor does the weakness of our nature make us easily defeated. Let no one think or persuade himself differently – nothing but our own vices have conquered us.

Salvian, *On the government of God* 7. 23

In the third century, catastrophes, both real and perceived, affected the psyche of the Roman people. It would be simplistic to claim that the shaking of the world order caused Romans to question and adapt their religion, because classical religion had no dogma; Roman religion was questioned and adapted throughout antiquity. The crises of the third century did not change this philosophy but rather accelerated and highlighted existing trends.

One such trend was 'orientalising', an expression used by historians for the 'eastern' influences of places such as Syria and Asia Minor on the traditions of the Roman Empire. It has been argued that this was increased by Julia Domna, the very influential Syrian wife of Septimius Severus. In this argument, orientalism played an increasing role as the third century progressed, leaving its mark on statuary, social customs and literary tradition. A counter-argument claims that 'orientalism' is so all-encompassing a term as to be meaningless. Furthermore, an objective study shows that eastern influences on Roman life were less pervasive than is sometimes claimed and were not always for the worse where they did occur. Once it is accepted that oriental influences per se are no bad thing, orientalism is no longer a symptom of decline.

Certainly, the third century saw the spread of 'eastern' religious beliefs, although it should be pointed out that the west was influenced by eastern religious beliefs long before the third century. Dionysus (Bacchus, in his Roman manifestation) was almost certainly imported from Asia Minor during the Archaic era, two thousand years before, and Cybele, the Magna Mater, was an eastern goddess whom the Romans deliberately imported in the late second century BCE. Therefore, one must regard with scepticism claims that the emperor Elagabalus was particularly orientalising when he brought his god El-Gabal to Rome and attempted to set it at the head of the Roman pantheon. El-Gabal was a sun god, a Syrian version of Helios, an established Roman deity. The very Roman cult of the sun as Sol Indiges was even older. Another popular mystic cult from the east was Mithraism,

New approaches to religion

'Western' emperors, such as Aurelian, were also sun-worshippers. This did not reflect orientalism but henotheism and syncretism. Henotheism is the near-exclusive worship of one god, while admitting the existence of others, where syncretism reflects the attempt to pull diverse forms of religious belief into a single intellectual framework. Neoplatonism, a mixture of philosophy and mysticism that became popular during the third century was a form of syncretism.

which became entrenched in the army and among members of the later Roman aristocracy.

Christianity, which taught that God was at once tripartate and a single deity, fitted in well with the overall trend in belief, just as the apocalyptic vision of Christianity suited the mood of the times. Christianity differed from contemporary religions in that it violently rejected all deities other than its own and preached that acceptance of other gods was a mortal sin. In itself 'sin', as opposed to normal wrongdoing, was a new concept to most Romans. The Christians' refusal to take part in state cult activities brought the religion's followers into conflict with the authorities. Those striving to hold together an empire coming apart at the seams had little patience with those who refused to participate in the religious ceremonies that were part of the empire's common cultural heritage and acted as a social binding mechanism.

Emperors may not have put their perception in those terms but they certainly saw Christians as a threat, hence the unprecedented Edict of Decius in 249 CE, which demanded that all citizens of the empire formally state that they had sacrificed to the gods. This was probably intended both to unite the empire in common religious activity and to expose those – that is the Christians – who did not participate. In Roman terms, the *pax deorum* was a compact by which the gods protected mankind in exchange for the performance of ritual and sacrifice. The

Christians' abandoning of those rituals and sacrifices affronted the gods and if enough people abandoned traditional worship the gods would withdraw their protection. As signs multiplied that the gods were doing exactly that, third-century emperors and local authorities became ever more savage in their persecution of Christians, not least because even atheistically inclined authorities realised that Christians were a convenient scapegoat. Nevertheless, Christianity continued to spread. It is now impossible to ascertain what proportion of the people were Christian and also certain that many of the versions of the 'Christian' religion as then practised hardly fit a modern definition. The religion took different forms in the east and west of the empire and schisms were frequent. The works of early writers such as Tertullian and Cyprian of Carthage were influential in standardising religious belief, while Christian prisoners of the Goths introduced their religion to their captors.

Imperial persecutions hit the church hard, but also reinforced the faith of believers and unified the church. Apart from the persecutions, the most significant developments in the Christian religion in this period were the assertion by Pope Stephen I (254–257) of the primacy of the Bishop of Rome and the development of monasticism. Organised single-sex religious communities developed in Egypt and spread to the rest of the empire during the medieval and late imperial eras.

5

Rome in late antiquity

The period of relative stability following the military anarchy of the third century is generally reckoned to be the achievement of three men. Aurelian (270–275) pulled together a disintegrating empire, Diocletian (284–305) stabilised the imperial succession and extensively reformed the administration of the empire and, Constantine the Great (306–337) implemented dramatic changes which set the tone for the era that followed.

The regnal dates of these emperors gloss over complex dynastic arrangements and succession struggles. Also assigning credit for the imperial recovery to these emperors gives insufficient credit to others, such as Philip the Arab and Decius who laid the groundwork for later success, or to social trends in the general population that allowed reforms to be implemented and succeed.

The imperial recovery

> After the successful ending of the wars we have fought, we must give thanks ... for the blessings of peace won with so great an effort.
>
> Edict of Diocletian CIL 5.3.801

One of the architects of the recovery, Diocletian, came to power in the traditional manner for a third-century soldier-emperor; he was acclaimed by the troops and then defeated and killed his predecessor. After his accession, Diocletian campaigned successfully on the Danube and in the east. The west, especially the defence of Gaul, was left to Maximian, a capable subordinate. To keep Maximian's loyalty, Diocletian set up a mechanism for the imperial succession, a belated recognition that the lack of one was the fatal flaw of the Roman Empire.

The Diocletianic succession mechanism became what is today called the Tetrarchy. The basic principle was that the troops of a successful general would not need to rebel to make him emperor, because the emperor would already have made that general his heir. Eventually Maximian was elevated to the rank of Augustus and co-emperor alongside Diocletian. Each 'Augustus' then nominated a 'Caesar' as his subordinate and successor. Thus, in 297 CE Diocletian (the Augustus in the east) dealt with a rebellion in Egypt while his Caesar, Galerius, campaigned successfully against the Persians. Maximian (the Augustus in the west) stamped out banditry, which had become a major problem, in Gaul, as Constantius (his Caesar), campaigned on the Rhine. For almost two decades the Tetrarchy gave the Roman administration stability and the breathing space to tackle its numerous problems.

Bureaucrats

Although it is a convenient shorthand 'bureaucracy' is a misnomer for the Roman administrative system. Properly speaking a bureaucracy is a corps of administrators, selected on ability and promoted on merit. In Rome, 'promotion' was not an accepted concept. People got jobs through favouritism and nepotism and rose through the ranks through patronage, bribery and the exchange of favours. This was not corruption, because 'corruption' implies another system is there to be corrupted. In Rome (and elsewhere) this *was* the system.

Diocletian greatly accelerated the imperial tendency to divide provinces into smaller administrative units. By the end of his reign there were over twice as many provinces within the imperial borders than had existed a century before. These were administered by a bureaucracy some ten times larger than that of the principate.

The provinces were grouped into larger units, *dioceses*, usually administered by a subordinate to the praetorian prefect. The few large military operations that were not commanded by one of the tetrarchs were conducted by a senior military officer, a *dux*, (whence the modern 'duke'), rather than by a provincial governor. The new regime increased the size of the army yet again and committed substantial resources to building extensive defensive lines and fortifications. To pay for them, a new form of property tax was introduced which valued land on its productive capacity; this was supplemented by a poll tax. The informal mechanism through which areas supporting a legion paid their taxes in kind to the legion was set on an unambiguous legal footing. Under Diocletian, a further attempt to increase revenue involved doubling the face value of coins and publishing a list of maximum prices for goods and services. This economically naive attempt at controlling inflation flew in the face of reality. The result was scarcities (where goods not worth selling were withdrawn) and a thriving black market. The edict has, however, given historians a handy guide to approximate minimum costs in the late third century.

Diocletian launched a persecution of the Christians, one of the few to be instituted across the empire. He put in place reforms that defined the role of provincial governors and collected codices of previous governmental edicts. In 305 Diocletian retired, making him the first emperor to leave the job alive. When he died in 312 his tetrarchic system did not long survive the removal of his powerful personality. It foundered because of power struggles among his successors, because the army preferred the dynastic principle of inheritance, and because Constantius, Maximian's newly appointed co-emperor, wanted to be succeeded by his son Constantine.

Constantine

> This thrice-blessed prince ... his conflicts and battles against the foe, his personal valour, his victories and successes in war and the many triumphs he won: also his care for the interests of individuals, his legislation for the social benefit of his people and so many more imperial labours.
>
> Eusebius Pamphilus, *Life of the Blessed Constantine* 1.11.1

Constantine, son of Constantius, was another of the 'soldier emperors' from the Illyrian and Danube regions. He was born in the frontier province of Moesia. His father, Constantius, served under both Aurelian and Diocletian before he became second-in-command and heir (the tetrarchic 'Caesar') to Diocletian's co-emperor, the 'Augustus' Maximian. As a young man, Constantine campaigned with his father in Britain against the Picts. Eventually, Diocletian resigned and forced Maximian to do likewise. This made Constantius Augustus in the west and Galerius (Diocletian's successor) Augustus in the east.

When his father died in 306, Constantine unilaterally assumed the rank of Augustus, which should have passed to an appointee of the current Augustus, Galerian. The ex-emperor Maximian had given up his imperial powers but, refusing to accept Constantine as his new ruler, attempted to retake power. In the battle for Rome that followed, Constantine ordered his soldiers to mark their shields with the *chi rho*, the symbol of Christ, a move that his followers claimed led to the defeat and death of Maxentius, Maximian's son. (Maximian later committed suicide on Constantine's orders.) This was the first step towards the Christianisation of the Roman Empire. However it is worth noting that Constantine's triumphal arch which still stands today beside the Colosseum in Rome was erected soon after Constantine took Rome. This arch bears classical references to the pagan gods but has no overtly Christian symbols.

We do not know to what extent Constantine was 'Christian' in the modern sense of the term. He was baptised on his deathbed, though this was not uncommon among contemporary Christians. His major contribution to Christianity was not that he was a follower of the religion but that in 313 CE he, and his co-emperor Licinius passed the famous Edict of Milan which ordered that 'Anyone who wishes to observe the Christian religion may do so freely and openly, without molestation.' Although this edict allowed Christianity official status within the Roman Empire, it is unlikely that Christianity was then the religion of the majority of the empire's citizens. Christianity was not to be the official state religion for another seventy years.

Constantine fought a series of campaigns against his rivals – including his co-emperor in the east – and ended as sole ruler of the empire, a move which ultimately destroyed the tetrarchic system. When he had consolidated his position, Constantine made a number of far-reaching reforms. One of the most dramatic was the stabilisation of the coinage. As he distanced himself from the classical religion of his ancestors, Constantine had fewer inhibitions about seizing the treasure which had accumulated for generations in the temples of the gods. The gold from the temple treasures was minted into coinage. A pound of gold became the *solidus,* which survived through various mutations to become the symbol for the (British) shilling, which only became obsolete in the late twentieth century, along with the '*d*' symbol for a penny, from the *denarius*.

After the legitimising of Christianity within the empire, perhaps the most significant of Constantine's measures was founding the city that bore his name until the 1920s. Constantine regarded Constantinople as his capital, although during his lifetime the city was generally referred to as the 'new' or 'second' Rome. Constantinople was built partly on the ancient Greek city of Byzantium, which is why that part of the Roman Empire which survived the fall of the west is today known as the Byzantine Empire. When Constantine died in 337 he left his successors a very different Roman Empire from that established by Augustus three hundred years before. In Augustus' day the city of Rome ruled an empire of different peoples and cultures; even in Italy there were independent tribes and some half a dozen separate major cultures. Constantine's sons ruled an empire in which citizens across the Mediterranean considered themselves Roman. Although local cultures and traditions remained firmly embedded beneath the Roman overlay, the peoples were united by common languages (Greek in the east and Latin in the west), a single legal code, a shared literary culture and a common architectural tradition. As time went on, the peoples of the Roman Empire came to share a single religion although there were regional variations on the common theme. However the Roman Empire of the fourth century shared the unresolved problems which had festered since the time of Augustus.

Constantine's succession had violated the tetrarchic system, so the succession issue remained a problem, but at least the constitutional position of the emperor was unambiguous. He was an absolute monarch above the law and able to legislate on his own authority. Although individual senators remained powerful and influential, the senate had become little more than the municipal council of the city of Rome.

Whereas the emperor had once pretended he was merely the first among equals (*princeps*) fifth-century emperors were explicitly masters (*domini*) of the empire, so this era is often called the 'Dominate'. Supreme power in the Dominate was passed by dynastic succession and as a stated principle rather than a de facto arrangement. This cleared the deliberate obfuscation of Augustus' era, but because any member of the imperial family was a potential successor to the current emperor, life became extremely hazardous for them. (Constantine executed his wife and one son.) The risk of summary execution for suspected treason made genuine treason almost an act of self-defence, a fact of which emperors were well aware and that ratcheted imperial paranoia up another notch.

Fertility rates in antiquity were low and many children died before reaching adulthood. Add to this the internecine tendencies of an imperial family and it becomes clear why most late imperial dynasties seldom lasted more than two or three generations. The end of every dynasty encouraged opportunist usurpers and wholesale political upheaval ending in civil war. Consequently the army remained a powerful political force. Rebellions and mutinies occurred every decade until the fall of the western empire. Also, although Constantine's commandeering of temple treasuries had solved the inflation issue, the empire still needed a larger army than Rome could afford. The economics of this period are even murkier and more hotly debated than those of earlier eras, but the empirical evidence is consistent with ever-increasing taxation chasing suppressed economic activity down an accelerating spiral of diminishing returns. Despite the efforts of revisionist historians, it is probable that the relative stability of the fourth and fifth centuries was not a return to prosperity but a period of remission before the empire in the west was swept away altogether.

This does not mean that late antiquity was a sterile prelude to the medieval era. Rather, it was a period of intense debate and inquiry which established many of the foundations of modern Europe and a period in which Christianity became the force that was to dominate the cultural and intellectual agenda for the next thousand years.

Christianity

> If you ask for your change, you'll get a sermon on the nature
> of the begotten and unbegotten. Ask for a loaf of bread and
> you'll be informed that 'the Father is the greater and the Son
> the lesser' and the maid who draws your bath will tell you that
> the Son was created from nothing.
>
> The popularisation of religious debate
> Gregory of Nyssa in *Patrologica Graeca* (writings of the Greek
> Church Fathers) 46.557

Before Christianity there were no 'pagans'. 'Pagan' simply meant
an outsider, someone apart from the traditions and jargon of a
particular group. City-dwellers and the military both called
outsiders 'pagans'. Cults such as that of Isis neither rejected other
religions nor defined themselves by that rejection; not until the
rise of Christianity did a spirit of 'us' against 'them' become a
major factor in religious discussion.

Our knowledge of religious debate in this period comes from
those who felt strongly enough to write about it. We have little
idea of how the average Roman viewed the arcana of Christian
debate or how important religious affiliation was in determining
social and political groupings. It is however clear that modern
nostalgia for the 'simpler' beliefs of early Christianity is misplaced.
From the very beginning Christianity was dogged with heresies
and schism; only during the fourth and fifth centuries were the
outlines of today's Christian dogma hammered out.

The composition of the Holy Trinity, and particularly God's
relationship with his 'son' Jesus, was hotly debated as was the
question of whether Jesus was human, divine or both. In one
corner the monophysites claimed that Jesus was purely divine, a
manifestation of God. In the opposite corner, followers of Arian-
ism (named after the Alexandrian preacher Arius, who taught in
the early fourth century) believed that Jesus was a separate being

created by God. Between these two poles lay (among others) Anomoeanism, Nestorianism and Eutychianism; creeds that attempted to bridge the gap between the more radical positions.

The Donatist controversy in North Africa resulted from the attempted Diocletianic persecution of 303. Donatists violently rejected those 'traitors' who compromised with the imperial authorities, even if they tried to return to the church. This had theological implications for the validity of penance and repentance, for the church was meant to accept the truly penitent, and ended with the Donatists being declared heretics. They were so harshly suppressed that even St Augustine of Hippo, one of the movement's harshest critics, was driven to protest. Hardly had the Donatist controversy died down than Augustine's doctrines were attacked from another direction by the 'British' monk Pelagius (Pelagius' allegedly British origins are unconfirmed). The Pelagsians queried the concept of original sin and the prevailing interpretation of free versus divine will. Pelagius was banished from Rome and vanishes from the historical record, though his arguments are still debated.

Church councils met frequently to thrash out the thornier issues dividing the Christian faith. Among the first was the council of Arles in 314, a meeting of religious authorities summoned by Constantine, which eventually excommunicated the Donatists. This was followed in 325 by the council of Nicaea, which defined Jesus as the son of God yet 'of one being with the father' (the dogma recited in mass today by Roman Catholics and other sects as the 'Nicene Creed'). This council also separated Easter from the Jewish Passover and attempted to set a common date for its celebration across Christendom. At the council of Nicaea both the Arian and Monophysite positions were rejected in favour of the middle ground, still determinedly held by the Catholic Church. Until the late fifteenth century this was simply 'the church'; it took the title 'Catholic' from the Latin *Catholicus* ('general' or 'universal') just as Protestant ideas began challenging it in western

Europe. A further series of councils in the late fourth century, held in Rome and Hippo (in north Africa), established the Gospels of Matthew, Mark, Luke and John as canonical, thus rejecting both a variety of other 'gospels' (henceforth called 'apocryphal') and those who wanted to accept only a single gospel.

In short, the basic tenets of modern Christian dogma were set in place not by disciples and apostles but in meetings of the leading intellectuals of the fourth century. Those whose theories came to dominate religious thought for the next thousand years are known as the church fathers and their writings as the Patristic texts. Chief among them were Origen of Alexandria, in the early third century; Gregory, bishop of Constantinople in the late fourth century; his contemporary, Gregory of Nyssa; Augustine of Hippo; and the mid-fifth century theologians Cyril of Alexandria and Nestorius.

Pagans and Christians

> Go, if you think it will do you any good, to the public altars and shrines and there perform your customary rites, for we do not forbid the rituals of previous times from being openly celebrated.
>
> Edict of Constantine to the pagans, 319 CE
> *Theodosian Code* 9.14

Throughout the later fourth century, opposition to Christianity continued, though it is uncertain and improbable that 'pagans' presented a united front to the new religion. Ecstatic religions such as the cult of Isis had as little in common with stolid worshippers of Jupiter as they did with Christians or the theorising Neoplatonists. As Christian influence spread through the hierarchy of imperial officialdom, many individuals probably converted less through conviction than as a pragmatic means of advancement or to avert perceived bias against themselves or their communities.

Pagans were briefly given hope that the Christianisation of the empire might be reversed by Julian (355–363), the last emperor of the Constantinian dynasty, who rejected Christianity in favour of Neoplatonism. However, it took some time for Julian to become established; for much of his 'rule' he was a junior emperor (Caesar), or co-emperor, according to the tetrarchic system, which by then was largely defunct. Once in supreme power Julian embarked on a campaign against the Persians in which he perished from a lance-thrust, which some improbable later accounts claim was inflicted by a Christian Roman soldier. After Julian's death all of Rome's emperors were Christian, in several instances devoutly so, and their example proved persuasive.

Certain milestones marked the Christianisation of the empire, including the Edict of Theodosius in 380, which made Christianity the state religion, the withdrawal of funding for pagan ceremonies and the banning of pagan displays in the 390s. This period saw the closure of the Serapaeum (a famous pagan shrine) in Alexandria and the suppression of the ancient Olympic Games as a pagan rite, probably in 435. Despite isolated attacks on pagan temples, forcible conversions and anti-pagan riots, the rhetoric of the church was generally more violent than the actual practice. In 415, the Neoplatonist, Hypatia of Alexandria was shamefully lynched by a mob of monks but such incidents were rare. Few prominent pagans were martyred specifically for their beliefs; in Hypatia's case misogyny played as big a part as religion. Generally, the population of the empire converted peacefully to the Christian religion over a period of 250 years.

Christianity introduced new concepts as well as that of 'pagans'. Pagans had generally left religious interpretation to individuals, with the implied assumption that the gods were perfectly capable of dealing with blasphemers. The Christian church introduced the concept of 'heresy', whereby deviation from established dogma was an offence against the church and increasingly, against the law. Other concepts now part of western culture became widespread at this time, for example the distinction between 'crime' – an offence against the secular authorities – and 'sin' – an offence against God. Likewise Christianity required 'faith' and 'belief' of its followers, whereas classical religion demanded only observance of religious rites. Some sociologists identify the development of a 'guilt' culture, in which individuals felt bad about wrongdoing itself, replacing a 'shame' culture with its fear of wrongdoing becoming public knowledge. Despite the enthusiastic adoption of Christianity by aristocratic women, the fourth and fifth-century church had a decidedly misogynistic bent. The church father Tertullian was not exceptional in bluntly calling women 'the devil's gateway' in his polemic *On the dress of women* (1.12). Women were fallen creatures thanks to the sin of Eve. Those women who did not submit to the rule of their husbands were not only committing a social offence (as always) but also sinning against the church.

Pagan priests had been active members of the political class but Christian clergy seldom held secular offices. However, aristocratic families generally placed members in positions of authority in both the secular and religious systems, not least because the church had huge moral authority. Having family connections in the clergy afforded some protection against charges of heresy, or practising magic or the Manichaean creed. Magic had been considered separate from religion since at least the first century BCE but was widely practised. In the late empire, practising magic was a crime punishable by death; a charge that became a convenient way to dispose of political rivals. Manichaeism was an oriental religion considered a rival creed to Christianity and was persecuted ever more fiercely as the century went on.

While intrepid bishops such as Ambrose of Milan were able to reproach emperors for misconduct, such men were exceptional. The emperors of late antiquity considered themselves

guardians and mentors of the church and controlled the administration and appointments of the clergy, just as they controlled
secular appointments. Nevertheless, the church had a separate
administrative structure and the sanction of divine punishment.
As the western empire collapsed, the church sometimes became
the only functioning authority in an area and temporarily the de
facto government.

Rank and position

Some people should not be considered credible witnesses, either
because they are in the power of others, because of the unreli-
ability of their judgement or because of the stigma and disgrace
of their type of life.

On the admissibility of testimony, *Digest of Justinian* 30.5

One effect of the rapidly-multiplying administrative offices of
the late empire was that status in Roman society became explicitly defined by official rank. With the proliferation of offices came
the customary abuses to which any civil service is prone: rent-
seeking, cronyism, bribery and the establishment of sinecures
were rife, and most officials took care to insulate their positions
from the civic duties and taxes that fell ever more heavily on the
few still liable to pay them.

The increased rapacity of officialdom reflected the need to
pay for the vastly expanded bureaucracy and army. There was
an ever-increasing trend for those in a position to escape taxation to do so by whatever means or influence they had. Those
who could not escape the impositions of the state were generally
known as *humiliores*, a term used to describe the 'more humble'
members of Roman society such as artisans, tradesmen and peasants. Their betters were, with considerably less accuracy, referred
to as *honestiores*. To a large extent this division of society was

more important than the division between slaves and free men. The poorest and most oppressed *humiliores* were for all practical purposes slaves. One reason for this was that immensely wealthy senators had huge rural estates. Workers on these estates were *coloni;* men legally bound to work the land, either as unfree labour or tied tenants, with little actual distinction between the two. A *colonus* who fled from his position was formally enslaved if captured.

While it is difficult to confirm from the patchy court records of this period, there seems to have been an increasing tendency to visit punishments formerly reserved for slaves – such as crucifixion or a messy death in the arena – on wrongdoers of low class. Despite the blurring of the line between *humiliores* and slaves, Roman society of this period was not only composed of have-not *humiliores* and rich *honestiores*. Many *humiliores* were quite well-to-do, and other classes such as the poorer clergy and the military, had legal and financial exemptions that placed them outside either of these two divisions. The record shows that those in slavery were considered a distinct and lesser class to even the poorest of the free, even if the reality did not reflect this. Often the fate of the very poor was not relegation to the rank of slave but exclusion from Roman society altogether. Since the Edict of Caracalla in 212, almost every free inhabitant of the Roman Empire had become a Roman citizen. Nevertheless, not all those living within the bounds of the empire were Roman; there was a substantial population of foreigners who had immigrated from outside the empire. Their numbers were enlarged by judicial decrees that removed citizenship from individuals and groups as a statutory punishment.

Other 'aliens' living alongside Romans within the empire included the families of *foederati*, barbarian troops who served with the imperial armies under their own commanders and fought in their native style. At the death of the general Stilicho there was a widespread, and officially encouraged, reaction against the barbarian population of many frontier and garrison towns which led to large-scale massacres. Barbarians not only lived within Rome's frontiers as individuals within towns, but also as complete communities largely insulated from Roman culture and law. The policy of allowing controlled admission of barbarian peoples within Rome's borders was a response to the growing pressure of migratory tribes on Rome's frontiers. This immigration policy was originally intended to supplement the citizenry of the frontier provinces and provide extra manpower for the army and agricultural sector. As time went on barbarian settlement within the empire became large-scale, more autonomous and further from the periphery, while barbarian leaders became ever more influential in imperial government.

The eastern and western empires

Thus the venerable city [of Rome] ... like a careful parent, wise and wealthy, has trusted the management of her legacy to the Caesars, as her children.

Ammianus Marcellinus 14.6.5

The tetrarchic system did not survive, but neither did the domination of the empire by a single ruler: governing and defending the empire was simply too complex a task. Rome's frontiers were under threat, from the 'Saxon Shore' in Britain, to invading Huns across Europe, to Persians in Armenia. The last emperor to rule the entire Roman Empire was Theodosius II (408–450). Yet Theodosius only won control over the western portion of the empire after he defeated the western usurper Joannes in 424. Rather than rule directly, Theodosius installed the six-year-old Valentinian III as western emperor.

Apart from growing cultural differences, both parts of the empire had developed separate military and administrative systems. Integration, even if it had been practical, would have had immense political repercussions for the upper classes, which based their struggles for power and prestige around one or other of the two systems. In comparison to the chaotic evidence for this period as a whole, we have a clear idea of the Roman administrative and military systems in the early fourth century thanks to a unique document, the *Notitia Dignitatum*. This is a detailed list of court officials, provincial governors and military commanders, including descriptions of the forces they commanded and where they were stationed. There are numerous problems with this document, both because of errors in the surviving copy and because the original may have described an ideal situation rather than reality. Nevertheless, the thousands of positions reflect how far the bureaucracy of the empire had changed from the principate, when Rome's domains were essentially governed by the senate and the emperor's household staff.

In the divided empire, the east steadily grew stronger than the west. There were two reasons for this; first, the east was easier to defend. The western empire's borders were the Rhine and the Danube rivers; barriers that were relatively easily breached. One of the most disastrous invasions suffered by the western empire came when a hard winter froze the Rhine and removed its defensive value altogether. In comparison, the heartlands of the eastern empire were in Anatolia. Asia Minor has seas on three sides and almost impassable mountains on the other while the Levant was guarded on the east by extensive tracts of desert. Even if heavily defended oases such as Palmyra and Dura-Europos could be taken by an eastern invader, the difficulty of maintaining extended supply lines meant that any Persian invasion was necessarily of limited duration and extent. The Persians had their own problems with barbarians (especially a group called the White Huns) and were consequently less aggressive than they had been in the third century. Finally Egypt was geographically inaccessible to any invader who had not conquered the Levant and was thus sheltered from the regular military crises which shook the rest of the empire.

More defensible frontiers meant fewer invasions and smaller and cheaper armies. This led to a stronger economy and a stronger economy led to greater prosperity, less support for usurpers and therefore fewer dynastic struggles. As far as can be seen from the archaeological and textual evidence, the later Roman Empire was positively thriving in places such as Antioch and the western Anatolian seaboard. The second reason for the greater strength of the eastern empire was that peace on the frontiers led to a modest revival in trade with the orient. The western empire was bordered by the sea and had only the scant trade opportunities offered by barbarian tribes. The eastern empire traded extensively with the great civilisations of Persia, India and China and imported spices and pepper from as far afield as Java. Many of these luxury goods eventually found their way to the aristocratic elite of the western empire, but the eastern empire was the west's only source of such goods. This left the west at an economic disadvantage, as it had little to offer in return other than cash. Consequently, money desperately needed by western armies went east to pay for luxury silks and spices for Rome's top senators and courtiers.

Since the western empire was relatively accessible to invasion and migration, many tribes, deflected by the relatively strong defences of the east, instead raided and settled in the west. Though the fall of the west is an immensely controversial and complex topic, there can be little dispute that the relative success of the eastern emperors against the barbarians ultimately determined the different fates of the two halves of the empire.

Barbarian invaders

I myself, once arrived at the palace gates to see barbarian envoys in attendance, each in his way gigantic, truculent and terrible, yet different in complexion ... beards, dress and hairstyles.

Eusebius Pamphilus, *Life of Blessed Constantine* 4.7.1ff

The common belief that in the fifth and sixth century the Roman Empire in the west collapsed under a wave of barbarian invasions is, at best, misleading. Although invasions irreparably strained both the economy and the social structure Rome was generally able to hold its ground militarily. However, this was due less to the competence of the Roman army than to the success of Roman diplomacy in co-opting various barbarian groups to fight on the side of Rome. The problem with this development was that the empire became increasingly dependent on barbarian military strength. Consequently 'barbarian' leaders rose in the Roman command structure until the western emperor became the puppet of barbarian generals. Once the position of emperor had lost its power, the final removal of the office had little effect on contemporary western society and politics.

The most influential of the tribes that so dramatically changed the fate of the western Roman Empire was a group of east Germanic peoples collectively known as the Goths. Not only were the Goths numerous and skilled fighters and diplomats but Roman dealings with them set the pattern for future interactions with other barbarian tribes. In part the Roman response to the Goths was dictated by precedents set in the centuries of warfare with the Germanic tribes beyond the Rhine, when the Romans had used the time-proven technique of divide and conquer, a judicious mix of bribery and coercion which persuaded some tribes to fight rival tribes, leaving Rome stronger than either.

What we know of the Goths from their own history comes from the sixth-century historian Jordanes. His history, the *Getica* describes how, over the centuries, the Goths migrated from southern Scandinavia to the lands between the Vistula River and the Black Sea. At this point, in 238 CE, Goths and Romans came into contact. Rome was gripped by its third-century crisis and a large-scale Gothic raid plundered the province of Moesia Inferior with relative impunity. The Roman response set the pattern, to some degree, for later events. Instead of responding with military force (which was not available), the Romans purchased back the prisoners taken by the Goths and then hired Gothic tribesmen to help with their wars in the east. Thereafter Goths and Romans sparred constantly on Rome's northern frontier. Some emperors, such as Decius (249–251), suffered significant defeats and some, such as Claudius Gothicus (268–270), won major victories (although both died on campaign against the Goths).

There were two important developments in the third century; the first was the conquest of Dacia by Gothic tribes, although it appears that both the Roman language and culture continued to thrive under the province's new masters. The second was the conversion of the Goths to Christianity, through active proselytising by missionaries and the influence of the many Christian captives taken in Gothic raids. Roman-Gothic relations changed dramatically with the arrival of the Huns. In what has memorably been described as 'the billiard ball theory of history', the impact of the Huns on the eastern lands of the Goths translated into Gothic pressure on the north-eastern Roman Empire. While many Gothic tribes were subjugated by the Huns, a large faction under the chieftains Alavivus and Fritigern decided to take their chances with Rome, and in 376 they petitioned the Romans for the right to settle within the imperial frontiers.

The emperor Valens agreed to their request in the hope that the refugees would provide the empire with farmers and eventually soldiers to shore up its depopulated frontiers. This technique had been used by the emperor Julian two decades before, when the Franks had been settled with some success along the Rhine. However, the Goths knew nothing of the techniques for avoiding a rapacious bureaucracy that Roman citizens had learned from necessity. The provincial administration where the Goths had settled concentrated on squeezing every last coin out of the newcomers, who were driven to extremes of poverty and desperation. Not unexpectedly, in 376, they rebelled.

Adrianople

An irredeemable disaster which cost the Roman state so dearly.

Ammianus Marcellinus on the battle of Adrianople
in 378, 31.13

After two years of indecisive fighting against the rebel Goths, the emperor Valens gathered a large army to resolve the matter. The alarmed Goths immediately proposed negotiations offering to stop fighting and remain peacefully within Roman frontiers. Valens, believing he had the superior army, opted to fight. The Gothic force fortified itself on a hillside behind its waggon train. Valens, misled by poor intelligence before the battle, failed to realise that most of the Gothic cavalry was away foraging. The cavalry returned while the Romans were attacking the waggons. The Roman cavalry put up a poor show and fled the field, leaving their infantry pinned at the foot of the hill, exhausted and hardly able to manoeuvre. The battle turned into a massacre, in the course of which Valens joined Decius in the gallery of Roman emperors killed by Goths.

The impact on the empire was devastating; most of an irreplaceable field army of veteran soldiers was destroyed. The north-eastern provinces were defenceless and only the walls of Constantinople, which guarded the crossing of the Bosporus, prevented the Goths from conquering much of the eastern empire. Valens' successor, Theodosius I (379–395) managed some minor successes against the Goths, and eventually agreed to more or less the terms offered to the Romans before Adrianople. The Goths settled within the empire under their own leaders and laws; when they fought for Rome they did so as *foederati*. The Roman administration might have seen this as a stop-gap measure to be rectified over time, but as the empire slowly fell back into crisis, the Gothic settlement became the standard model for assimilating barbarians within the empire.

Alaric the Goth

I have overrun peoples and cities, I have burst through the Alps and drunk the waters of the river Eridanus from a victor's helmet. What is left for me [to conquer] but Rome?

Speech of the Gothic king Alaric in Claudian's
On the Gothic War 205

The Frankish *foederati* produced two capable leaders who rose high in the Roman military administration, first Richomer and later Flavius Arbogast. Arbogast became so powerful in the west that he either killed the reigning emperor Valentinian II, or drove him to suicide. Flavius Arbogast was a barbarian – that is, a non-Roman – and so could not make himself emperor. Instead, he selected a court official, Eugenius, a former grammarian and schoolteacher, as his proxy. Eugenius' promotion to the imperial throne in 392 marked the beginning of a process in which powerful leaders with barbarian backgrounds were the real rulers of the western empire.

In response to Valentinian's death, Theodosius marched westward in 394. The climactic battle of the brief campaign took place at the River Frigidus (the Wippach, on the border between modern Italy and Slovenia). As Arbogast and Eugenius were believed to be pro-pagan, later Christian propaganda claimed that Theodosius' victory was that of the true faith over the powers of darkness, although there is little evidence that contemporaries saw the battle this way.

Theodosius installed his younger son Honorius as emperor in the west and returned to Constantinople, where he died the following year. This left Honorius and his competent subordinate Stilicho to deal with their disaffected Gothic *foederati*. Alaric, king of the Goths – or at least of a substantial portion of the branch known as Visigoths – had fought at the Frigidus and was bitter at the way his tribesmen had (possibly intentionally) been thrown into the thick of the fight, suffering heavy casualties. Disappointed that the sacrifice of his tribesmen brought little recognition from the authorities, Alaric turned rogue. In the last years of the fourth century he made a massive raid on Greece which devastated Corinth, Argos and Sparta. Despite this attack, and an attempt to do the same in Italy that was thwarted by Stilicho at the battle of Pollentia in 402, Alaric never became totally alienated from the Roman authorities. They continued to grant him various titles and allowed him to become the de facto governor of Illyria.

Stilicho, unlike many Romans of the day, recognised that his first priority was to maintain his army as a fighting force, because destroying it to win a splendid victory over one enemy would leave the western empire defenceless against others. Therefore, he bribed and conciliated Alaric whenever possible. This was not popular to people brought up on tales of Roman military prowess; Stilicho lost so much political support that his enemies were able to persuade Honorius to order his execution in 408.

The Vandals and the Huns

> My voice sticks in my throat and sobs choke my words as I dictate. The city which conquered the world has itself fallen.
>
> Jerome to Principia letter 127.12, describing
> the sack of Rome

Stilicho had encouraged barbarian units to join the Roman army; many deserted to Alaric on news of Stilicho's execution. With a large and motivated army behind him, Alaric promptly marched on Rome, where Honorius vacillated between appeasement and treachery. Although later historians have criticised him for indecision, the truth is that he had very little to bargain with. He had withdrawn his court to the safety of the marshes of Ravenna and although he was personally safe, he had neither the soldiers to eject Alaric from Italy nor the money to buy him off.

The Romans of the city bought some time by raising the funds to appease Alaric. However, in 410, after a brief siege the barbarian leader captured and sacked Rome. As sacks go this was a positively humane affair, with minimal damage to either population or the buildings of the city. Nevertheless, the event sent shock waves around the empire; this was the first time that Rome had fallen to barbarians since the Gallic sack in 390 BCE, seven centuries earlier. Although Alaric had been in Italy for almost two years before he took Rome, little help for the beleaguered city had arrived from the rest of the empire, much of which had problems of its own. Alaric's Goths did not have the resources to hold Rome; after the sack they moved on. They eventually ended up in Gaul, establishing a kingdom around Tolosa (Toulouse) which lasted beyond the fall of the western empire.

In 406, the Franks defending Gaul came into violent contact with another wave of invaders; the Vandals. They, allied with a tribe called the Alans, crossed the Rhine – possibly while it was frozen – and after temporarily subjugating the Franks proceeded to devastate Gaul. (This invasion contributed to the downfall of the half-Vandal general, Stilicho.) The Vandals eventually moved on through Iberia to settle around Carthage, in Africa, in some of the richest lands of the empire. The Vandal occupation of Carthage may not have been entirely unwelcome to a local population alienated by the insatiable demands of the imperial bureaucracy. However, for the authorities in Rome the loss of Carthage represented a substantial loss of revenue. Under their enterprising king, Genseric, the Vandals not only kept the Roman army at bay but also expanded their dominions into a tidy little kingdom comprising most of the former province of Africa Proconsularis.

The Vandals steadily expanded from their African base; in the years approaching the mid-fifth century they regularly raided

Sicily and the coast of Italy. In the last year of his rule the emperor Valentinian III (423–455) offered his daughter in marriage to Genseric in exchange for political and military support. This support was both needed and too late, for Valentinian was assassinated soon afterwards. The Vandals nevertheless came to Italy and captured and sacked Rome. This sack was more violent and sustained than Alaric's and when the Vandals departed they took the former emperor's daughters with them.

Today the term 'vandalism' is synonymous with mindless destruction, a reputation bestowed on the Vandal tribe by contemporary writers. However, the archaeological record suggests that there was continuity rather than destruction in lands occupied by the Vandals, so this reputation may be undeserved. The Vandal kingdom in Africa lasted beyond the end of the western empire until 534, when it was conquered by the eastern Roman Empire.

The Vandals and Goths were not alone. In the fifth century, the western empire contained a number of autonomous barbarian tribes, including the Franks in north-western Gaul and the Suei in Spain. A trend established under Stilicho became more entrenched. The emperor ceased to command armies in person. As the fifth century went on, real power in the west was drawn into the hands of the leading military commanders, the *magistri militum*. These commanders increasingly set policy and managed diplomatic and administrative affairs, reducing the emperor to a figurehead. Perhaps the most important role of these men was to balance the conflicting priorities of empire and barbarians and to co-ordinate the efforts of both groups to repel further waves of barbarians.

The most powerful of these *duces et patricii*, or patricians, was Flavius Aetius, who dominated the west from 430 until his assassination in 453. During his early career Aetius fought the Franks and Visigoths and frequently skirmished with Bonifacius, the commander of Africa, who eventually succumbed to the

Figure 6 Stilicho as depicted in a famous diptych in Monza Cathedral in Italy. (The other panel of the diptych depicts Stilicho's wife Serena and his son Eucherius.) (Picture P. Matyszak)

Vandal invasion. However, Aetius is generally judged by his later campaign against one of the greatest threats to the later Roman Empire: Attila the Hun. One of his victims had titled Attila 'The Scourge of God', an epithet he cheerfully adopted. During his reign the Huns dominated a vast tract of land from the Urals to the Roman frontier.

Huns and White Huns

The Huns of Attila appear to have been a different people to the mysterious 'White Huns' or Hephthalites. The historian Eusebius says that the latter got their name because they were paler than Attila's Huns and did not mix with them. The White Huns put considerable pressure on the Sassanian Empire and occupied part of its territory.

This was fortunate for Rome as the west was fully occupied with Attila and other problems and a Sassanian invasion might have been devastating.

Attila first challenged the Sassanian Empire to the east but he was defeated in Armenia. He probed westward until he found the relatively weak frontier defences of the Danube. A series of military confrontations demonstrated that the Roman infantry offered little in answer to the fast-moving and ferocious Hun mounted archers. The Hunnic drive eastward from the Danube was thwarted by the walls of Constantinople, so Attila turned west. Valentinian III still held the throne in the west and Aetius was his *magister militum*. Aetius had briefly lived among the Huns, having been sent to them after being held hostage by the Gothic king, Alaric. Genseric, the Vandal king, shared a powerful dislike of the Goths with the Romans, so it was natural for Aetius and Genseric to combine forces against Attila. Matters were then complicated by Honoria, Valentinian's sister. Honoria's mother, the formidable Galla Placidia, had arranged for her to marry a Roman senator. Deeply averse to the idea, Honoria appealed to Attila for help. Attila chose to interpret this as an offer of marriage and promptly accepted, claiming half the Roman Empire in the west as his dowry. In 451, the Huns attacked, ostensibly to intervene in a power struggle among the Franks. The Romans and Visigoths allied against them as the Huns plundered their way towards Orleans. The invasion was stopped on 20 September, at the Catalunian fields, in a massive battle that saw Attila defeated

Figure 7 Pope Leo I meets Attila the Hun, as imagined by the painter Francesco Solimena (1657-1747), in a painting now in the Pinacoteca di Brera, Milan, Italy. In reality Leo was probably less influential in changing Attilla's mind than the plague and dilapidated state of Italy.

and Theodoric, the Visigoth king, killed. It is possible that Aetius refrained from following up his victory and adding Attila's name to the casualty list because he saw the Huns as an essential counterbalance to the Visigoths.

Attila had not given up on Honoria and her 'dowry'. In 452 he attacked again; this time the target was Italy. With his army crippled by plague, Aetius could neither defend the Alpine passes nor field enough soldiers to stop the Hunnic threat. Just when it appeared inevitable that Rome would be sacked, Attila turned back. Despite the claim that the personal intervention of Pope (properly described at this time as the 'Bishop of Rome') Leo I had persuaded the invaders against desecrating the eternal city, it is more likely that Attila's army was also suffering from the plague. Furthermore, Italy had suffered so much in recent decades that there was little left to plunder.

Within two years of this event all the main protagonists were dead. Attila died, either from internal bleeding or possibly simple over indulgence on his wedding night. Valentinian III decided that his *magister militum* was becoming too powerful and personally killed him; a move famously described as 'cutting off his right hand with his left'. Valentinian attempted to ally with the Vandals but before this alliance was consummated he was killed by aggrieved former supporters of Aetius. Amid the chaos following the deaths of Aetius and Valentinian III, a Visigothic aristocrat Ricimer rose to become the new patrician and de facto ruler of what remained of the western Roman Empire. Since a non-citizen 'barbarian' could not be emperor, Ricimer placed a series of puppet rulers on the imperial throne. These puppet emperors occasionally displayed a distressing independence which generally led to their deaths and replacement. Ricimer was the last effective ruler of the western empire. When he died (probably from the plague) in 472, he was followed by weak and ineffectual emperors culminating in the young Romulus, nicknamed Augustulus ('little Augustus'). When, in 476, the patrician who was the power behind Romulus Augustulus was deposed in a military coup, Augustulus was not considered significant enough to merit execution. Rome's last emperor was bundled off into monastic retirement. The new patrician, Odoacer, had barely the military and political support needed to hold Italy. Pragmatically, he let the rest of the western empire go its own way. The west was by now at best a loose commonwealth of autonomous tribes, so

The Rome that did not fall

Although 476 saw the end of the western Roman Empire, the eastern empire continued for almost a thousand years, until the last remnants were destroyed by the Ottoman Turks, who sacked Constantinople in 1453. Many of the 'last Romans' who fled the Turks moved to Italy; some historians credit the new thinking that they brought with them for sowing the seeds of the Renaissance.

this involved no actual administrative change and had almost no impact on day-to-day life.

Odoacer did not formally dissolve the western Roman Empire; instead he sent the last emperor's regalia to Zeno I, emperor of the east. Technically, Rome's empire was reunited under a single ruler but practically, the western empire had ceased to exist.

Epilogue

Though the fall of the last emperor of the west, in 476 CE, is generally considered the end of the Roman Empire, this is not how it was seen at the time. That year was not regarded as particularly momentous by most people living in the west. Other than – technically – being brought under the suzerainty of the emperor in the east, life continued as normal for the former subjects of the western empire. Those liable for taxes continued to pay them to the local authorities and those subject to Roman law in 475 continued so to be in 477. The 'fall' of the west was certainly not a single cataclysmic event; rather, a further stage in a centuries-long transformation.

It has been argued that perceptions of the catastrophic fall of Rome and the dark ages that followed are unduly influenced by British historians. Certainly, from the perspective of the ancient Britons the end of the empire was indeed as catastrophic as the aftermath was dark. However, in other regions, such as Iberia and Italy, evolution rather than collapse marked the transition from late antiquity to the early medieval period.

Furthermore, for many of its subjects, the Roman Empire continued. What modern convention calls 'the Byzantine Empire' was still known to those living under its rule as the Roman Empire. At its greatest extent, in the middle of the sixth century, the Byzantine Empire included Italy and parts of Spain and Africa, as well as the traditional lands of the eastern Roman Empire in Greece, Egypt and Anatolia. If one were to look for the final catastrophic fall of the Roman Empire, one would have to look to the capture of Constantinople by the Ottoman Turks almost a thousand years later.

If we accept the traditional Roman date for the foundation of Rome which, despite healthy scepticism, historians have never actually been able to disprove, we have a very exact set of dates for the biography of Rome and its empire. According to the Roman historian Terentius Varro, Rome was founded on 21 April, 753 BCE. Oddly enough, other accounts dispute the year but not the month or day. The birth date of the Roman Empire is generally considered to be 722 years later, when Octavian, later known as Augustus, took control of the Roman world, on 2 September 31 BCE. From then, Rome was ruled by emperors, until 4 September 476 CE, when the last western emperor was deposed. The eastern 'Byzantine' Empire held on to its diminishing domains until 29 May 1453. Rome lasted an epic 2,206 years (and one month and eight days), of which only 507 years, or just under a quarter, are conventionally described as the period of the 'Roman Empire'.

Those five hundred years influenced Europe and western culture more than any period until, arguably, our own. Above all, the Christian church was nurtured within the Roman Empire. Throughout the Medieval period, the religion's headquarters were in Rome (as the Roman Catholic Church's is today). During the Dark Ages the church was almost the only organised structure in many areas, and for most of the Medieval period was the only functional transnational organisation of any note. The influence of the Christian church on Europe, and on the world, is so immense as to be incalculable, yet it can be argued that without the Roman Empire, it might not have existed at all.

Although Latin fragmented, its successors, the Romance languages (Romanian, Italian, Spanish, French and Portuguese), are not only recognisably close to one another but after English are among the most widely spoken languages in the world. Likewise, one of the great feats of late antiquity, the compilation of Roman law into the single framework of the *Code of Justinian*, laid the legal framework that has endured in Europe until modern times. Indeed, praetors served as minor magistrates in Rome until 1998.

Nor did the political structure of Rome pass unremembered. That fact that Europe had once been united under a single power led to periodic attempts to repeat the process. For a while, the Byzantine Empire existed alongside the Holy Roman Empire in central Europe. The Holy Roman Empire lasted from 962 to 1806, despite being acidly described by Voltaire (in his *Essai sur l'histoire générale et sur les mœurs et l'esprit des nations* Ch.70) as 'Neither holy, Roman, nor an empire'. The French Empire, which the emperor Napoleon consciously based on the Roman model, starting his career in power as 'first consul' of the French Republic in 1799, came later. Other attempts at empire building to evoke ancient Rome included the short-lived regimes of Hitler and Mussolini. A more fitting tribute to Rome's contribution to European unity is the Treaty of Rome, signed in 1957, which laid the foundations of what is today the European Union.

Nor has the influence of Rome been confined to Europe. It has been argued that the Caliphate of the early Muslim Empire has an equal right to be recognised as a successor to the Roman Empire along with those other heirs, Byzantium and the Catholic Church. Rome's influence can be seen in governments around the world, especially those that include a Senate, such as the United States of America. At the time of the founding fathers, the work of the Roman historian Plutarch was second in popularity only to the Bible, and the constitution of the United States consciously drew on the Roman Republic for its inspiration. This has been noted by some critics, who claim that the USA is now replicating some of the late Roman Republic's flaws.

In short, this epilogue is not an epitaph for the Roman Empire, for it has not died. In law, language, architecture, religion, art and culture, Rome is very much still with us today.

Timeline

The Regnal and Republican eras

753	BCE	Traditional date of foundation of Rome
612	BCE	Fall of the Assyrian Empire
50	BCE	Rome's last king expelled, Rome becomes a Republic
390	BCE	Rome defeated and occupied by Gallic invaders
282–272	BCE	Rome defeats King Pyrrhus of Epirus
264–241	BCE	First Punic War
218–201	BCE	The second ('Hannibalic') Punic war
216	BCE	Romans defeated at the battle of Cannae
206	BCE	Rome defeats Carthage to become the dominant power in Iberia
202	BCE	Hannibal defeated at Zama (in North Africa). Carthage surrenders
200–197	BCE	Rome attacks Carthage's former ally, Macedonia
192–188	BCE	Roman war with the Seleucid Empire
191	BCE	Antiochus III of Seleucia defeated at Thermopylae and driven from Greece
189	BCE	Roman victory at the battle of Magnesia in Asia Minor cripples the Seleucids

171–168	BCE	Third Macedonian war ends with the Roman partition of Macedon
146	BCE	Rome sacks and destroys Carthage Rome destroys Corinth, Greece becomes a province
133	BCE	King Attalus dies, leaving the kingdom of Pergamon to Rome Death of Tiberius Gracchus, social reformer
121	BCE	Killing of Gaius Gracchus reveals major social divisions in Rome
112–106	BCE	War with Jugurtha ends with Roman control of Numidia
102	BCE	Huge Germanic invasion finally thrown back at the battle of Aquae Sextiae
91	BCE	Start of the 'Social war' as Italians demand Roman citizenship
89–85	BCE	War with Mithridates in Asia Minor
88	BCE	Sulla leads a Roman army to take Rome
73–71	BCE	Third Servile war – including uprisings led by Spartacus
73–63	BCE	Pompey defeats Mithridates and conquers Jerusalem
69	BCE	Roman army victorious at Tigranocerta in Armenia
63	BCE	Marcus Tullius Cicero becomes consul of Rome, defeats Catiline conspiracy
58–50	BCE	Caesar conquers Gaul
53	BCE	Crassus dies at Carrhae attempting to defeat the Parthian Empire

49–45	BCE	Caesar crosses the Rubicon, defeats Pompey in Greece and becomes dictator
47	BCE	Cleopatra takes power in Egypt as a Roman client
44	BCE	Julius Caesar assassinated in the senate
43	BCE	Octavian joins forces with Antony and Lepidus to form the triumvirate
31	BCE	Octavian victorious at the battle of Actium

The Principate

27	BCE	Octavian awarded the title Augustus by the senate
		Augustus' 'first settlement' resolves immediate crises facing the empire
23	BCE	Augustus almost dies, 'second settlement' outlines the emperor's powers
6	CE	Augustus establishes the *aerarium militare* – the military treasury of Rome
7	CE	Augustus adopts Tiberius
9	CE	Massive rebellion in the Balkans, three legions lost in Germany
14	CE	Augustus dies, Tiberius establishes the first imperial succession
32	CE	Jesus Christ executed
37–41	CE	Caius Caligula's reign. Caligula is the first emperor to die violently
44	CE	The emperor Claudius begins the conquest of Britain
54	CE	Nero becomes emperor

60–61	CE	Revolt and death of Queen Boudicca of the Iceni
64	CE	Rome devastated by a huge fire, first persecution of Christians
66	CE	Rebellion in Judea
68	CE	Revolts against Nero in Gaul and Hispania
69	CE	Year of the four emperors
79	CE	Herculaneum and Pompeii buried by the eruption of Vesuvius

The 'High Empire'

106	CE	Trajan conquers Dacia
122	CE	Work starts on Hadrian's Wall in Britannia
132	CE	Bar Kokhba uprising in Judea
161–180	CE	Reign of Marcus Aurelius, increasing barbarian pressure on the frontier
180	CE	Foundation of the Sassanian Empire begins over a century of warfare
193–211	CE	Reign of Septimius Severus
212	CE	Edict of Caracalla extends Roman citizenship to all free people of the empire

The third-century crisis

217	CE	Macrinus becomes the first non-senatorial emperor
235	CE	Maximus Thrax becomes the first emperor never to see Rome
247	CE	Emperor Philip the Arab leads celebrations of Rome's first thousand years

249	CE	Edict of Decius begins an empire-wide persecution of Christians
260	CE	Emperor Valerian dies as a Persian captive
260	CE	Roman Empire nearly breaks into three
270	CE	Emperor Claudius Gothicus dies; Aurelian comes to power and reunites the empire
284	CE	Diocletian becomes emperor
305	CE	Emperor Diocletian retires, establishes the 'tetrarchic system'

The Late Empire

306	CE	Constantine declares himself Augustus
313	CE	Edict of Milan allows Christians freedom of worship
324	CE	Constantine establishes his eastern capital at Constantinople
376	CE	Goths under Alavivus and Fritigern petition to settle within the Roman Empire
378	CE	Emperor Valens defeated by the Goths at Adrianople, dies in battle
379	CE	Theodosius I becomes emperor – the last to rule east and west
380	CE	Edict of Theodosius makes Christianity the state religion
402	CE	Stilicho defeats at Alaric at Pollentia
408	CE	Stilicho executed by order of Honorius Theodosius II becomes emperor of the east, aged 7
410	CE	Alaric sacks Rome

415	CE	Hypatia of Alexandria lynched
435	CE	Suppression of the ancient Olympic Games as a 'pagan' festival
451	CE	Attila the Hun is defeated by Visigoths and Romans at the Catalaunian fields
454	CE	Assassination of Aetius, the last great Roman general in the west
455	CE	The Vandal sack of Rome
476	CE	Romulus Augustulus deposed, Odoacer takes control of Italy. End of the western Roman Empire
1453	CE	End of the eastern Roman Empire

Further Reading

General

The most definitive texts on the Roman Empire are *The Cambridge Ancient History* series (CAH) vols 8–14. These are regularly updated to include the latest archaeological and scholarly research. Also recommended is *The Oxford History of the Classical World* (1989), which puts Roman civilization in context with other periods. Another good, though slightly dated, book is H. H. Scullard's *A History of the Roman World* (1980).

Specific Periods

The crisis of the Republic is well explained in Tom Holland's *Rubicon* (2005), which can be read in conjunction with Syme's landmark book *The Roman Revolution* (2002). A. Everitt's biography *Augustus: The Life of Rome's First Emperor* (2007) describes the situation in the early imperial period. Matyszak's *The Sons of Caesar* (2006) gives the lives of the later Julio-Claudian emperors. The third century crisis is well-summarized by Pat Southern in *The Roman Empire from Severus to Constantine* (2001), while Brown's *The Making of Late Antiquity* (1978) should be read together with A. Cameron's *The Mediterranean World in Late Antiquity* (2011).

Military

Adrian Goldsworthy's *The Roman Army at War* (1998) gives a solid theoretical background, while Matyszak's *Legionary* (2009) gives details of service in the Roman army. The Osprey series *Rome's Enemies* gives descriptions of the many different peoples Rome fought in different eras, while Luttwak's *The Grand Strategy of the Roman Empire* (1979) remains a provocative 'must-read' text.

Source Books

These books give selected original texts from antiquity, which illustrate life in the ancient world. Lewis and Reinhold's two volumes of *Roman Civilization: Selected Readings* (1990) give texts from the Republic and Imperial eras, while Jo-Ann Shelton's *As the Romans Did* (1998) gives an eclectic look at the Romans in their own words. *Handbook to Life in Ancient Rome* (1998) by Lesley and Roy Adkins gives lists of everything from distances between cities to Roman weights and measures. Suzanne Dixon's *Reading Roman Women* (2001) provides a look at Roman women from original sources.

Economy and Society

R. Hughes, *Rome: A Cultural, Visual, and Personal History* (2011) provides useful insights. J. Carcopino's book *Daily Life in Ancient Rome* (1962) is a classic study, which might be read in conjunction with Matyszak's lighter text *Ancient Rome on Five Denarii a Day* (2008). A more academic study of the wider empire can be found in P. Garnsey and R. Saller, *The Roman Empire: Economy, Society, and Culture* (1987). Sarah B. Pomeroy's *Goddesses, Whores, Wives, and Slaves: Women in Classical Antiquity* (1975) tells the story of Roman women in the empire and contrasts this with other women in the ancient world.

Archaeology

A good introduction to the topic is Binford's *In Pursuit of the Past: Decoding the Archaeological Record* (1983), while Bodel's *Epigraphic Evidence: Ancient History from Inscriptions* (2001) offers insight into a topic that is ever more influential in modern studies of antiquity. Hölscher's *The Language of Images in Roman Art* (2004) is a useful guide to understanding statuary, and Alcock and Osborne's *Classical Archaeology* (2007) gives a good overview of the empire and beyond. A good case-study for the general reader is Mary Beard's *Pompeii: The Life of a Roman Town* (2010). For Rome specifically Platner and Ashby, *A Topographical Dictionary of Ancient Rome* (1929) remains the definitive guide, though this is a dense text best suited for specialists. For those specifically interested in Roman coins, David Sear's *Roman Coins and Their Values* (1988) is again the definitive text.

Entertainment

Donald G. Kyle's *Spectacles of Death in Ancient Rome* (1998) is a recommended text, which puts the arena into its social context, while Wiedemann's *Emperors and Gladiators* (1992) explains the purpose of gladiatorial spectacles. *Roman Circuses: Arenas for Chariot Racing* (1986) by John H. Humphrey is a good introduction to the subject. For less violent entertainment Richard C. Beacham's *The Roman Theatre and Its Audience* (1992) is recommended.

Ancient Sources

Given the huge number of extant texts even some important authors have been omitted. The selected reading is intended to give an example of the huge variety of texts available to the general reader, both in the original and in translation.

Historians

These are the main writers of our period, but not the only ones. Minor historians such as Dionysius of Halicarnassus and Velleius Paterculus are more often used by specialist scholars.

Polybius   A Greek who saw Rome both as an insider and as a foreigner. His history is accurate, but limited to the mid-Republic when Rome became an imperial power. He was extensively used by Livy.

Livy   His famous history of Rome started with the foundation and carried on down to his day, but unfortunately the later books are lost, and we have only a brief summary of Livy's history of the Late Republic.

Caesar   A first-person history by one of Rome's great imperialists. Caesar's description of his conquest of Gaul has been a standard Latin text for schoolboys almost from the day he wrote it until today.

Appian   Writing some time after the events he describes, Appian is a solid historian who draws on sources now lost. Apart from a history of the wars of the dynasts he wrote separate histories of some of Rome's expansionist wars.

Tacitus   An intelligent, acerbic historian, quick with opinions and epigrams, and the best historian of the early imperial era. His remains the definitive history of the early Julio-Claudian emperors.

Cassius Dio   A Roman senator who wrote in the time of the emperor Commodus. He adds extra detail which complements existing histories, and provides a fresh perspective. His history has many gaps, but it originally covered the story of the empire to his own time.

Ammianus Marcellinus   Sometimes called the last great historian of Rome. His history takes us through major events of the later empire such as the reign of Julian the Apostate, the last pagan emperor, and the crucial battle of Adrianople.

Biographers

Suetonius His lives of the twelve Caesars are not only a useful historical resource, but also fascinating reading in themselves.

Plutarch His biographies are well-researched and immensely influential even today. Regrettably most of his subjects are from the mid-to-late Republic, rather than the imperial era.

The Augustan histories a compilation sometimes called 'the Lives of the later Caesars'. A scurrilous collection of texts under a variety of pen names. Written with sensationalism in mind, these histories are as reliable as the worst of gossip magazines, but are still all that historians sometimes have to go on.

Philosophers

Those interested in this topic should consider the following.

Cicero When excluded from politics, Cicero wrote works such as 'On the nature of the Gods' and 'On old Age'. These give insights into the Roman perception of how the universe operated.

Lucretius His epic poem *De Rerum Natura* ('On the nature of things') remains one of the great Roman philosophical texts.

Epictetus A stoic and freed slave, Epictetus has opinions and ideas that are still fresh and challenging today.

Marcus Aurelius the *Meditations* are a must-read text. A Roman emperor telling us – in his own words – what he thinks of life the universe and everything.

Poets and novelists

There is a huge wealth of Latin literature – only some of the major names can be touched on here.

Virgil Though other sets of poems such as the *Eclogues* are very readable, Virgil's master-work was the *Aeneid*, a text which told Romans old and new what it was to be Roman.

Ovid   Light-hearted, occasionally scurrilous, Ovid is a poet who can still be read for pleasure today.

Martial   A satirist of the first century AD. His verses are touching, humorous, outrageous or perceptive in turn. Be wary of letting minors read an unexpurgated edition. Few topics are taboo to this writer.

Horace   A prolific writer. His poems give a wealth of information about life and attitudes in the Augustan age.

Apuleius   Writer of one of the two novels to survive from antiquity. (The other is the *Satyricon*). His book the *Golden Ass* gives many incidental details about life in second-century Greece.

Letter writers

Cicero   All Roman aristocrats were indefatigable correspondents, and we have Cicero's mail preserved in such detail that it is sometimes possible to follow the events he describes almost day-to-day.

Seneca   A philosopher heavily involved in imperial politics, Seneca's letters are sometimes sententious, and at other times packed with useful insights.

Pliny   Writing with publication in mind, Pliny the younger gives a lively picture of his life and times, including a graphic description of the eruption of Pompeii, written for his friend Tacitus.

Other texts

This is an eclectic selection which illustrates various aspects of the Roman Empire at different times.

The New Testament   Even if it were not arguably the most important religious text ever written, the New Testament would be valuable as one of the few texts written from a provincial viewpoint about life under Roman rule.

Pausanias   One of the first tourist guides ever written, his description of the Greece of his day gives an enduring and highly detailed description of a single region, town-by-town.

Pliny the Elder   *The Natural History* is a grab-bag of anecdotes, Roman science, geography and biology. Pliny was interested in anything and everything, and managed to record a lot of it in this epic work.

Vegetius   *On Military Matters*. Vegetius was interested in army reform in the late imperial era. His treatise tells us much about how the later Roman army functioned, and his comparisons give insights into earlier eras as well.

Priscus   The embassy. This is a diary-style account of a late Roman official who goes on a diplomatic mission to Attila the Hun and tells of the meeting in his own words. Another must-read text.

Index

Texts